Placed: An Encyclopedia of Central Oregon, Vol. 1

PLACED

An Encyclopedia of Central Oregon, Vol. I

Edited by Irene Cooper & Ellen Santasiero

Kairos Press Northwest
Bend, Oregon

ISBN 978-0-578-76105-3

Library of Congress Control Number: 2020919952

Cover artwork: Brigitte Lewis
Cover Design: Lieve Maas

Kairos Press Northwest
2580 NE Community Lane
Bend, Oregon 97701 USA

www.kairospressnorthwest.com
www.irenecooperwrites.com
www.ellensantasiero.com

Printed in the United States of America

First Printing, 2020

Acknowledgements

First and foremost, the editors thank the writers whose work appears in this volume. For the contributions of time, patience, good will, and well-chosen words, they are ever grateful.

They extend heartfelt thanks to: Sarah Cyr, Cat Finney, and Shelby Little, who helped conceive of this project and lay its groundwork; Jackson's Corner East for meeting space and a menu they never tired of; Brigitte Lewis for the beautiful cover art; Lieve Maas for her design and production expertise; and last but not least, the friends and family who have supported them these many months.

Introduction to

Placed: An Encyclopedia of Central Oregon, Vol. 1

At a Bend Public Library-sponsored (read: *free*) work-shop, then-Oregon poet laureate Kim Stafford slipped participants Irene Cooper and Sarah Cyr a small pam-phlet-style book about creating a document of place in one's community. A big part of the poet laureate gig is to plant these sorts of seeds, get things growing in some way across the State. Though the famous Poet is an af-fable fellow and an engaging teacher of ample charm, neither Sarah nor Irene were so naïve as to think such a project would simply and magically come together, knew such an endeavor would require significantly more organization and effort, than, say, getting the kitchen or a bedroom painted over the weekend, or, closer to the concept, planning a block party.

Both women, both writers, understood immediately that if they undertook such a project, they'd want it to reflect a wider swath of community than is addressed by the pro-motion of our region as a recreational destination, as a place to play. Which, of course, it is—but people (and a litany of other organisms) live here, too. Beyond craft brew and cold brew, they were eager to collect personal expressions of central Oregon in as much variation as possible. The concept was intriguing, and they were in. Also, they were savvy enough to enlist help.

In May of 2019, Sarah, Irene, Cat Finney, Shelby Little, and Ellen Santasiero sat around what had become the Friday morning community writing table at Jackson's Corner East and dreamed the dream. We divvied the tasks. We'd call it an encyclopedia, but keep it loose. We'd limit the length of the pieces, but not the forms they could take. We'd put out the call.

Cat created a website. Ellen got us a Gmail account. We drafted our email, and extended our invitations. We received responses, and questions, and more responses, and no response. When the pieces began to roll in, we had stories, explorations, travelogues, dispatches, hard data, poems. We continued to seek out the diverse community we sought to include. We extended our deadlines. We lifted our limitations on length. We brainstormed how to connect with contributors.

Abruptly, it was March 2020. No more Fridays at Jackson's Corner. No more meetings at Ellen's house. And as weeks and more weeks and months passed, our project, centered on the experience of central Oregon, lost its place along with its momentum. COVID-19 had, overnight, changed our relationship to place and to one another. We were tangled in an election year, and people were putting on masks and not putting on masks and taking to the streets to protest and demonstrate after the homicidal death of George Floyd. Our world had become both very, very big and very, very insular. We were in a different place, in our own places, looking out a window, staring at a screen.

But we had all these terrific pieces: a poem that attends to the auditory nature of the area; an informative lyric on wildfire; a thoughtful consideration of local food. We lacked submissions, still, from significant segments of the community we'd hoped to include. Our collection of pieces, diverse in voice and tone, was by no means an exhaustive representation. The editorial staff was trimmed to two—Ellen Santasiero and Irene Cooper. When the choice was made to pull this project into its physical reality, we agreed to start from where we were, and move ahead.

With a nod from our cohort, we reassessed, and reached out. We crunched the numbers. We adjusted our perspective. We'd get as close as we could. *Placed* would be a snapshot of our recent and far away before, and a reflection of this current liminal space, this very particular and endlessly variable corridor. We hope it is both meditation on and artifact of where we've been, and that it enriches the conversation of how we consider this place and our place in it, in the moment. We're different now. And we're here.

So, with the help of many, we made a thing, and we're calling it, Volume One. Our thanks to all contributors and co-conspirators, present and future.

~Irene Cooper & Ellen Santasiero, 2020

A

Amplify: *verb:* to make a sound louder

Bend's First Poetry Slam

It was a late evening in the early aughts at the Grove Bar in Bend when seventeen poets got up, one by one, squinted into a red Klieg light, and performed their work at the town's first Poetry Slam, a lively competitive event that uses volunteer audience members as judges. We heard rants and chants, odes and yawps, coming-of-age shticks and even a villanelle. We were asked to consider cigarettes, Illinois train tracks, tongues, Nevada highways, and peepshows.

We hooted and clapped for our favorite contenders, drink and dirty words flowed, and organizers divvied up the door proceeds into envelopes for the cash prizes. When one of the poets asked the crowd, "Should I read a mellow poem or an angry one?" the crowd roared, "Angry!"

During the break, a man with a whiskey in one hand climbed up on stage and took the mike. He was not one of the readers that evening. He told us he was a visitor from Chicago and that he wanted to say a few things to the people of Bend. Bend was off the hook, he said, when it came to beer, food, and women. He told us he liked being the only black person around here. He said, "Here they say, look, a real black person! out of curiosity." As it happened, our visitor wasn't the only black person around here--indeed, one of the finalists in the Slam, a young man with dreads tucked under his hat, was also black. The visitor rambled on some, and then gave up the microphone. Soon after, we all splashed into the final round.

When the man with the dreads took the mike, he smiled at the man from Chicago. He gave him a friendly hand gesture, and said, "I'll even read my poem like a brother." He started to read a poem about belonging and not belonging, about how it feels to live in a place where no one looks or sounds like you. When he got to a line in his poem that read, "like me," as in "there are people around here like me," he shouted the line and paused. Without missing a beat the visitor's voice shot back from the bar, "like me!" Again the poet called "like me!" Again the visitor responded "like me!" It was as if they were the only two people in the room.

At the end of the night another organizer praised the event, saying, "I don't know if I would call it the literary revolution, but ...." I wouldn't call it that either, but it was indicative of an evolving literary scene in Bend that included hundreds of writers working alone, and more and more venues where writers could share their work with others. Though the Slam bore only the slightest resemblance to a church meeting, it prompted the woman next to me to quip, "This is like a Baptist funeral, you never know what's going to happen."

~Ellen Santasiero

A

Asylum: *noun:* a place of refuge or protection; the state of being protected

Asylum

In November 2018, our coalition of faith-based groups in Deschutes, Jefferson, and Crook counties heard that an asylum family from Honduras, a couple with a young child, got permission to cross the border and would be staying with friends in Prineville. We were excited.

Our group is organized to be allies with our Latinx friends and neighbors who are under aggressive pressure from Immigration Customs Enforcement. Our mission is to get to know each other better and to create friendships with Latinx families whose culture and numbers have grown strong in central Oregon. We take direction from the Latino Community Association. Some of us have been trained to walk the court system with those who request support, some are advocating for immigrant rights, and some offer intercambio meals and hospitality.

Asylum is serious business. What kind of danger and heartache had required this family to flee family and country? With help from a bilingual mentor, we learned of the murders of a father, a sister and a brother-in-law, and a home reduced to ashes. We learned of threats of death and fire if the family didn't turn themselves over to armed men. We learned they had to make the terrible decision to flee, to sell all, to leave jobs and education, family, friends, and familiarity to seek protection in the strongest, richest, land of law that has always shown welcome and compassion for those whose lives hung by a thread. As we traveled with this family to Medford and Portland for required monthly visits, anticipated court outcomes, and helped them with daily living, our understanding grew and our lives were enriched by our friendship with this courageous family. And we shared their joy! Their second baby was born in central Oregon … on the 4th of July!

~Janet Whitney

B

Biennial: *adjective:* happening once every two years

Pandora Moth Hatch @ Vince Genna Stadium: phenomenon occurring in odd-numbered years, during which a large population of Pandora pinemoth (Coloradia pandora), for a brief period of time, congregate around the lights, screens, and fences of Vince Genna Stadium during the Bend Elks baseball season.

Five Cinquain Poems for the Pandora Moth Hatch @ Vince Genna Stadium

pinemoths
blotting the glare
couldn't care less about
a shut-out or extra innings
just sex

winged
caterpillar
shaped like a catcher's mitt
abandoned in the dust behind
home plate

Paiute
supplemental
treat, piuga, fat on
pine, roasted like peanuts. larva-
licious

pumice
your bed of choice
sleep drily for a year
before landing in a pint of
Bud Light

he grabs
the snow blower
and limp carcasses take
flight again, salt-flecked with fallen
pretzel

~Irene Cooper

B

Burn: *verb:* to combust or shine

Wildfire

Places have their particular catastrophe. Florida has hurricanes. The Midwest has tornadoes. California has earthquakes. In this corner of the world we are gluttons for disaster, primed for earthquakes, the stretch and yawn of dormant volcanoes, and most of all, the wildfire's white plume and red glow.

In August, skies grows hazy and sunsets turn red. Smoke hovers on the horizon, a dirty fingerprint swiped along the edge of the world. After enough time in the West, we know enough to see it coming, grass turning to crisp straw and the asphalt baking. After the Camp Fire and Mendocino Complex in California, after the Eagle Creek fire jumping the Columbia Gorge, we cannot deny the power of a stray ember, carried aloft like a firefly in the night.

We treat fire as our disaster. But trying to control it in the face of our fears only made it worse.

***

In 1911, the nascent Forest Service was tasked with fighting wildfires, beginning a century of well-intentioned suppression in a historically fire-managed landscape. As in all great tragedies, our struggle against fire led only to its intensification. Suppression over the past century has resulted in crowded, overgrown forests and fuel loads that burn hotter and longer, searing the landscape with the rage of an old god.

History tells us that, prior to suppression, central Oregon's dry forests burned frequently but with a light touch, as fire pared back the understory while allowing most trees to survive. Lightning struck and fires fed across the land, burning in mosaic patterns that prevented overcrowding or the spread of disease. Pine cones blossomed in the heat, releasing seeds that would germinate in the years to come. The forests followed an endless self-regulation with no ultimate purpose, a slow and pervasive change operating across centuries and millennia. Forests did this—they do this—on temporal scales beyond man's best-laid plans and busy calendars. The true settlers of the Americas, arriving thousands of years ago, knew the lessons we have just begun to relearn: there is no Oregon without fire.

We have put ourselves first in our narrative of the forests, naming them, mapping them, and extending the dubious protection of fire suppression to rangeland, campgrounds, trails, communication towers, springs, miles of board feet; elk, deer, turkey, trout; hunters, hikers, foragers. We have been drawn in by rivers and mountains, huckleberries and game, pooling around our forests like dew drops on a spiderweb.

There is no undoing the effects of the last century, although policy and management have changed in tandem with our understanding of forests and fire. We no longer stamp out every flame. We let some fires lick their way along the understory, skirting the bases of trees. Sometimes, in some places, the forest can still manage itself. We have to meet it halfway: begin to manage ourselves. The forest will do what it has always done, without intent or malice. We can work with fire, not just against it. If we continue to live here—and there's no stopping us—we'd do well to remember that.

Wildfires do not know where the forest ends and private property begins. They cannot distinguish between pine needles below trees and those caught in gutters. As with all catastrophes, fires do not discriminate.

***

The forest will burn. It will be healthy, if it can. It will be a wild, natural thing. We love the forest for the things it gives us, and fear it for the flames that threaten us, choke our air, darken our skies, snake their way toward our homes.

We cannot have one without the other. We may not love the fires, but in loving the forests, we must accept them. They burned before us. They burn around us. And no matter our policies, hopes, or efforts, they will continue to burn. They must.

The land of milk and honey has been prophesied across every corner of America, even in our sagebrush deserts and ashen soils. It is time to abandon our original myths; accept the land for what it is, what it always has been. Wild. Subject to fire. Dependent on it.

We live in the West. We live with fire.

~Anastasia Lugo-Mendez

"There's no Ethiopian food, and no Ikea."

—Melanie Fisher, co-owner of Cog Wild Cycling. "Bend, Ore., ... the city you'll love to hate," by Nathan Borchelt, *The Washington Post*, 5 Oct. 2012. Accessed 14 Sept. 2020.

C

Care: *noun:* systematic attention to restoring or maintaining health, treatment

Volunteers in Medicine

Volunteers in Medicine of the Cascades (VIM) is a place where the best aspects of the Bend community all come together. Medical Director John Letovsky describes it as, "Our community caring for our community."

Located across from St. Charles Medical Center (SCMC), VIM has provided free medical care since 2004 to more than 10,000 members of our community who are medically uninsured or critically underserved. Thanks to the coordination of a fiercely dedicated paid staff of 12, VIM functions mostly through the efforts of over 200 volunteers at any one time, donating their expertise as doctors, nurses, therapists, interpreters, pharmacists, healthcare educators, as well as administrative and IT specialists.

The first VIM clinic opened in 1993 in Hilton Head, South Carolina. The idea originated with Dr. Jack McConnell's picking up a hitchhiker, learning that the man and his wife were expecting a baby and they had no health insurance. Dr. McConnell had recently retired from a successful medical career and was tiring of his life playing golf. He gathered a group of other retired physicians, and they eventually opened a clinic assuring free health care for the Hilton Head community. That clinic has served as a model for almost 100 similar clinics nationwide.

About 90% of VIM patients in Bend are Spanish speaking immigrants. All patients find meeting monthly insurance premiums prohibitive, some losing coverage mid-year due to a job loss. The vast majority of these patients contribute to the local economy through their hard work in construction, restaurant work, landscaping, childcare, manufacturing, and housekeeping. By providing access to primary medical care, VIM serves to keep those of our community without access to health insurance from having to seek non-emergency services in SCMC's emergency room. Not only does that save space in the ER for patients with true emergencies, but it also helps otherwise uninsured patients stay on top of chronic conditions such as diabetes and high blood pressure. Consequently, should VIM patients ever need genuine emergency care, their medical issues are not compounded by neglected chronic conditions. Many local small businesses that are unable to offer health insurance also appreciate how VIM contributes to keeping their valuable employees healthy.

But VIM cannot do it alone. "We're not VIM without our community partners who provide specialty care pro bono," says Salome Chauncey, VIM's Referral Coordinator. These partners include cardiologists, surgeons, OB-GYNs, dentists and ophthalmologists, just to name a few. Of all the VIM clinics nationwide, Bend's VIM has one of the nation's strongest collaborations with such community partners, says Katherine Mastrangelo, Executive Director.

Why volunteer? For many healthcare professionals, volunteering periodically keeps their skills fresh, and many retired people value the vibrant collegiality and diverse community at VIM. Mastrangelo adds, "For those who are in the process of getting trained in the medical field, at VIM they can get valuable practical experience."

When volunteers are asked why they contribute time to VIM, responses include: *It's a place of joy ... There's a great opportunity to offer comprehensive, not strictly siloed healthcare ... I get to educate patients to help them reach their healthcare goals ... Such a wide variety of people come together for a common purpose ...* and *... For what I learn from the patients.* But the most common first response? *It's fun!*

~Ginny Contento

C

Croak: *noun:* a low, gritty sound

Great Basin spadefoot toads live in a variety of habitats in western North America but are one of the few amphibians found in sagebrush ecosystems. This toad uses a unique "spade" on its hind foot to dig deep burrows into the soil. Spadefoot toads are mostly nocturnal and they're most active after it rains and when humidity levels are high.

The Toad Queen

The ground trembled beneath a stunted sagebrush shrub. The Toad Queen emerged from her burrow to a changed world. Clouds of wildfire smoke hung over the landscape. Twisted ancient juniper trees burning nearby filled the air with an acrid aroma. A gust of wind pushed the flames across a bunchgrass meadow.

The Great Basin spadefoot toad gazed at this new world through her golden slitted eyes. Sand tumbled off her pale green spotted back. The Toad Queen stretched out a hind leg and shook soil off the dark spade on her webbed foot. Her sharp spades helped her dig a deep burrow in the gravelly desert terrain.

A tall larkspur plant stood near her burrow in a patch of smoldering bunchgrass. Its purple trumpet-shaped flowers drooped in the blistering heat.

A meadowlark perched on a bitterbrush shrub and sang to the Toad Queen. Dusty gray ash muted the brilliant yellow of his breast. He stopped in mid-song, interrupted by a fit of coughing, and then flew toward clearer skies.

"What happened while I slept in my burrow?" Toad Queen asked. She glanced around at the bleak landscape.

She and the other spadefoot toads pulled moisture from the soil when they slept underground and they survived the fire. Other creatures had not been so lucky. The carcass of a sage sparrow fledgling lay near her. A few feathers clung to the tiny dried-out body.

"A fire is taking our ancestral lands," her mate said. He emerged from his own burrow. The toad shook the sand off the black spades on his hind feet.

"The hot summer sun dried the plants of the steppe, and the fire will spread fast," she said. "We must call for help!"

Her mate called the other spadefoot toads. His loud croaking call carried far over the desert. At first there was no response, so he sang louder.

As he sang, a great horned owl suddenly swooped towards him. He and the Toad Queen retreated into their burrows. Once the threat passed, they emerged, and he resumed his singing. Toads in the distance joined him in song.

Dark clouds collected over the smoky skies. Billowy clouds accumulated into a towering thunderhead that produced a gentle shower of rain. The patter of rainfall on the earth woke other spadefoot toads. The toads emerged from their burrows and soon a loud chorus of croaks surrounded them. Lightning slashed across the sky and the air crackled with the energy created by their song.

The rain shower turned into a pounding downpour, and it doused the fires. Spirals of white smoke rose from the smoldering desert and drifted into the dark skies. The toads continued singing until the rain extinguished the fire.

"Thank you," the Toad Queen said. She beamed at the group of spadefoot toads gathered around her in a circle. They nodded their heads in unison toward their queen and called in duck-like notes.

The meadowlark alighted on the bitterbrush beside the Toad Queen. His melodic song of gratitude blended with the toads' voices and echoed across the countryside.

"Renewal will come to this land," The Toad Queen said. "But it will take time."

~Siobhan Sullivan

D

Day Trip: *noun:* a journey out and back that takes a day or less to complete

Rivering

It's high time we use river as a verb. "I am going to river today." Meaning one can engage in some activity around the flowing body of water. "What's on your agenda today?" "Just some rivering this afternoon." This could mean: kayaking, tubing, paddle boarding, board surfing, hiking, or just picnicking down by the river.

I rivered to Dillon Falls the first week of August 2020. This was my first visit to Dillon Falls. A beautiful metallic photograph capturing a copse of quaking aspens taken at Dillon Falls was my initial awareness of the area. I was eager to see the falls. I am not an outdoors person. I am more of a flaneur, who naively went to Dillon Falls expecting to see a modest waterfall flowing over a cliff. I won't be fooled again.

Its name is a bit of a misnomer. The falls were named after Leander Dillon, a nearby homesteader, who died in 1907. Why him and not another settler, I didn't find an answer. To be clear, there is no waterfall. Dillon Falls is one relatively small but thrilling portion of the Deschutes River. The Dillon Falls area is a sonorous and puissant Class V whitewater rapids section.

For context regarding rapids, there are six levels of classification for rapids. The International Rating system classifies them as follows: Class A - Lake water; Class I - Easy; Class II - Moderate; Class III - Moderately difficult; Class IV - Difficult; Class V - Extremely difficult; Class VI - Extraordinarily difficult.

I contentedly followed the easily marked paths. Walkers and bikers share the trail and then diverge with large Forest Service-constructed steps leading toward a narrower hiker's trail. The bike trail that I innocently followed walking down stream in my search for a waterfall is wider and a bit further away from the water. The hiker's trail that I followed on my return trip is closer to the water and has areas that are shady and tropical looking. At one point picturesque cliffs along and above the walking path are blanketed with moss and fallen pine needles providing a more mystical or magical backdrop.

Tire tracks were visible on the hiking trail as were shoe prints on the biking path. Anyone I encountered was friendly and courteous. During the week before noon, it was not crowded. As I was leaving around lunch time more cars were heading in.

Directions from the US Forest Service: From Bend, travel 7.9 miles west on Cascade Lakes Highway (46), then 2.6 miles south on Forest Road 41. At this junction there are signs to direct you to Dillon Falls. Before going to river at Dillon Falls, a parking pass is required, and they are not available at the site.

~Randy Workman

D

Dust: *noun:* fine particulate matter

Dust, smell of

Driving back to Bend, we're one of the few cars with the windows down, and the only one built after 1996. I always drive with the windows down. It's some remnant from a childhood spent with 4x40 air-conditioning (that's all four windows open and driving forty miles per hour, for those of you too young or too rich to know. We rolled our windows down in those days.) With the windows down, I can smell the places I drive past: the cattle farms, the gravel plants, the pine woods, the Valley. Columbus, Ohio was ozone, fresh-cut grass, hops, and car exhaust—a stale smell, like that stale city, like my stale self after a day of driving: eight hours back from Madison, Wisconsin by way of Chicago. But it was, for better or worse, the smell of home, resurrecting my childhood an hour before I arrived, whenever I reached the green sign that read, Plain City 1 Mile. Now that my mom has passed, I don't go back often. But when I do, it is the smell that first gets me—that brings the tears to my eyes.

Whenever we return to Bend, Oregon, the smell is the stony smell of the dust that coats everything in the summer: the lawn-chairs, the porch swing, the dining room table, the TV, the stereo, the dresser in my bedroom, the wood floors. The dust is equal parts basalt, ponderosa, and juniper; seasoned with manzanita, red ant, and horse manure. It coats the trails that we hike, is kicked up by the shuffling tread of my eight-, nine-, ten-year-old so that I walk thirty feet behind him when we hike the trails above Tumalo Falls. It doesn't matter. The dust stains my sinuses. It dyes my snot gray, but I don't mind it. The smell of dust transports me from my childhood to my son's childhood—from what was, to what is, to what could be.

~Ben Paulus

"I had been hearing on-the-ground buzz
that white folks were moving to places like Bend,
Oregon, ... That led me to discover through
census data that these towns were already
extremely white and they were becoming,
in most cases, even whiter."

—Richard Benjamin. "Journey into the Heart of Whiteness." *Mother Jones,* 23 Dec. 2009. Accessed 14 Sept. 2020.

E

Ear: *noun:* organ of hearing and balance in humans and other vertebrates; and, an ability to recognize, appreciate, and reproduce sounds, esp. music

SONOS

I capture sounds for future use:

> rubber on various forms of gravel, dust, sand,
> > and dirt
> mountains singing in the sun, rain, stars
> insects of calling varieties
> metal spoons softly scraping on titanium mugs
> conversations of two cyclists debriefing or
> > planning the days
> wailing of pain
> whispers of ghosts
> grasses in the wind
> pine needles crunching
> dripping sap
> metal on metal
> water in various forms

river rocks
splashing of river crossings
ocean waves
wind caught in fabric
skin on skin
typing an email—home
gasps of fright
static electricity
thunder in many forms
shotguns
pounding pavement
footsteps at various speeds
hum of air conditioners
horizons

~Alex Borgen

E

Equus: *noun:* genus comprised of horses, donkeys, and zebras

wild horse: noun: 1: an undomesticated horse (as Przhevalski's horse); 2: a feral domestic horse

Wild Horse

Wild horses gather at the clearing just 30 feet from where we are hiking. The Ochocos are filled with a magic of their own. We yell for our off-leash dog to return immediately, while she's unsure what to think of this pack of horses. The reality that they were wild and untamed took moments to become our truth. We only see horses in stables and horses with riders but here—just beyond those trees—five, now huddled together, not interested in our dog's attention. "Nacho"—we call her back in concern for her safety—does she understand these horses are *wild?*

Do I understand these horses are wild and free? My mother-in-law owns two in a stable not far from Sisters Rodeo. I ride her Morgan sometimes and help around the stable gathering new hay, carrying the new 50 lb block of salt from her red SUV to the center of the corral. I like to think they love me as much if not more than I love them. I like to think the way to be loved by my husband's mother is to love her horses, be dutiful and earn it.

The wild horses aren't living to earn love. How are they staying alive, I can't help thinking, as if all animals need humans to protect and care for them. Does free equal happier? Unmoored to another human's care and feeding schedule. They are following natural instincts that have kept them alive out here in the West for centuries. We hook Nacho's leash back onto her orange collar—matched to her brown fur, brown eyes, all over her shades of brown to match the fauna.

We stand alone in the Ochocos now, just a few birds fly overhead. Our understanding of the world, how nature is going along without us sinks down from the trees. We can either love them or not; the metaphor becomes clear.

-Amy J. Doherty

F

Fanged: *adjective:* to have sharp teeth

Mountain lion: also known as cougar, puma, panther, and catamount

Mountain Lion

I walk alone near Steins Pillar, a thumb of volcanic rock jutting out over private property in the Mill Creek drainage. The steep rock faces and boulders the size of elephants provide overhangs, shadows, cool places to wait. The light is dappled and hazy, the forest quiet, muted. The trail is empty. If it were to happen, I think, it would happen here.

I wait for the lion.

Lions are majestic and dramatic and destined to exist in television screens. As a child, I'd watch them yawning on an African savanna far removed from my existence.

It was during my first time out west, living in the Four Corners region of Colorado, that mountain lions became part of my reality. The warnings posted on bulletin boards at work warned me to be large, to stand my ground. Look them in the eye and don't run. I lived where I worked, in a storage shed converted to fit four bunk beds, three of which remained empty. I slept in one and piled the others with the belongings I could fit into a suitcase. In the evenings, I sprayed peppermint tea around the room, having heard spiders despised the smell, believing in it as a sort of magic, a protective charm against a host of new dangers.

In my previous home in New York City, I'd been afraid of third rails and muggings, car accidents and the looming shadow of terrorism. The list of threats here was different, wild and primal: lions, black widows, scorpions, rattlesnakes that sunned themselves on trails. I walked to my shed in the evenings with a flashlight aimed at the sagebrush on the hillside. If the light reflected green eyes back at me, I would know I was not alone. I stood at my front door and turned the doorknob, convinced that a lion waited within.

The next year, a wildlife biologist laughed at my fear. A mountain lion wouldn't eat me, because humans just don't taste good. But I knew as a small woman in a large forest, I would be an anomaly, a curiosity. I would be toyed with.

I feared lions when I worked in the woods, and I feared them when I ran the road from my cabin into town. The steep, rocky hillside hid a predator, and I imagined being ambushed. I imagined falling, and fighting, and scrambling for a rock, a stick, a weapon. I imagined protecting myself. I was in greater danger of being run over by a log truck than of facing a mountain lion. I was in greater danger of practically anything than a mountain lion.

It's been almost a decade since I stood at the door of my home and feared a lion within. I have yet to see one, but I haven't stopped looking. When I hike, a near daily occurrence on my job, I glance over my shoulder, peering up at the trees, into the shadows. I remind myself that I would not taste good. I am not that much of a curiosity. I am not worth a lion's time. This has never stopped my fear.

There will be a day that I am hurt. It may be in a car accident, or after a fall, at the hands of a stranger, or at the hands of someone I trust. It may happen with intent or without, in an instant or building up with the slow step of time. What I fear is that the thing that hurts me will not have been built to hurt me. The hurt will be without reason, unpredictable, arbitrary. I cannot protect myself against those things I cannot understand.

I wait for the lion, my old fear, feeling now that I know its place, its actions. The quiet of its steps, the curiosity or hunger that will drive it to me. I can protect myself against little else, but this—this I can understand. When the lion finds me, it will be here.

I will name it. I will face it. I will fight.

~Anastasia Lugo-Mendez

F

Flaneur: *noun:* a (hu)man who saunters; flaneuse (feminine)

Street Poetry Instigations are initiated outside of contexts where poetry is traditionally read or heard. Short poems are offered to passersby in public places, thereby exposing a broad cross-section of folks to poetry. This public service is undertaken by a poetry instigator who's moved by three passions:

1. Reading, writing, or sharing poetry.
2. Making offers of poetry sans expectation of recipients.
3. Engaging in spontaneous encounters with strangers.

Anyone of like mind can commence to instigating. The enterprise requires no university degrees, publications, permissions, or licenses.

History

Since April 2011, instigator "K." has handed out poems in public on *Poem in Your Pocket Day* during *National Poetry Month*. In April 2019, instigation frequency skyrocketed from once a year to every Wednesday afternoon in downtown Bend, Oregon. K. has no known co-instigators at present.

Elements of an Instigation

The instigator crafts a poem one week, selects one by another poet the next, and so on. Copies made, the instigator heads out with a photo-taking device [see Social Media].

Poems are brief and accessible; humor is not uncommon. Folks who *don't get poetry* may start to get poetry.

The stack of poems is given away in under 30 minutes. As passersby dash, stride, stroll, limp, lope, strut, trudge, and totter by, the instigator extends the poem, saying: *A wee poem for your pocket?*

Encounter is not urged, but rather encouraged by virtue of the instigator's visible, friendly presence in a hustle-bustle location.

No permits are required since nothing is being sold.

Social Media

A photo is taken of instigator and receptive recipient [sometimes, a four-legged] holding the poem. Photo and poem are posted to social media, whereby poetry is further spread.

Recipients

Delivery folks, meter readers, hippies, police officers, skateboarders, adolescents, business owners, workers, bent-over grandmas, stoners, homeless folks, families, locals, dogs, cats, visitors, artists, musicians, athletes, etc., of diverse gender orientations and socio-political-economic-ethnic backgrounds. Racial diversity remains limited in Bend.

The instigator has a delivery route to downtown businesses, wherein, owners and/or employees enjoy adding the weekly poem to their growing collections.

Responses

While research shows talking with strangers can boost a mood, most folks resist doing so. Folks can be wary; they've no idea the instigator isn't out to sell or preach.

The passerby is, likewise, a stranger to the instigator, who can't know why folks respond as they do. A poetry instigator takes responses in stride. Broad categories include:

No/Back Off: Polite decliners, outright ignorers, and wide swath-cutters [common among cell phone schmoozers]; all are sincerely thanked as they hurry by.

Maybe: The cautious-yet-curious quickly understand what's up. *Maybe* becomes *Yes.* Recipients light up, gladly take a poem, perhaps chat a bit and move on.

Definitely Yes: Enthusiastic receivers open their hands the moment they hear, *Poem for your pocket?* They eagerly talk poetry. Some recite or ask to hear the poem read aloud on the spot.

Four-leggeds are singled out here for their consistently receptive attitudes.

Vignettes of Encounter

Poems are offered to the quiet, loud, bubbly, downcast, receptive, guarded, and incoherent. Encounters can be funny, disquieting, sweet, poignant:

A disheveled man with matted hair, asked if he'd like a poem, rambles unintelligibly then suddenly says, *I'll take one,* and shuffles off.

An exuberant twenty-something wants extra poems for her AA compadres. A man heading to LA to make a hip-hop recording accepts a poem, then lays down some dance-inducing original rhymes.

A man, garbed in workout clothes, runs by: *No thanks, I'm all sweaty.* Uttered by someone in a thick parka: *Thanks, but I'm stuffed.*

At least once a week: *Is it religious?* The instigator suggests they decide. Most leave, poem in hand. There is the exceedingly rare trash toss.

Gifts

Some recipients want to reciprocate: they sing, dance, play instruments, share pastries, hugs, empanadas, M&Ms. Some read poems they've written. Occasionally humorous, most are characterized by gravitas and vulnerability:

A woman reads her poem about homelessness and her longing for empathy. A self-described *outsider to poetry* shares his first poem about being gay and his traumatic coming out. A young man makes a plea, slam style, for solidarity in response to corporate greed.

These encounters, placing an instigator in the role of witness, testify to the human desire for self-expression, a receptive listener, and connection.

Not All Roses

Within Bend's social stratosphere are folks burdened by poverty, mental illness, addictions, trauma, and homelessness:

Born with fetal alcohol syndrome, a woman lives a life of constant challenges on the street. A man mired in a bureaucratic mess can't get his medications. A couple's tent is stolen and with that, their protection from the elements. A savvy 29 year old woman, on the streets since age 14 to escape sexual abuse, is terribly lonely.

These folks, who said Yes to a poem, talked of deprivation, hopes, desires. An instigator has no ready solution, thus can only listen with care and interest. Instigators must be prepared to accept that sorrow is part of the landscape.

One may ask: Is there any point to offering poetry-as-gift to people living with such hardship? Maybe not. Yet though the ages, people enduring hardship have always turned to poetry. So the answer may be yes.

Philosophy

Poetry instigations are, fundamentally, a vehicle for relationship. Mutuality, intrinsic to encounter, dissolves the fictional line between giver and receiver. Instigator and recipient meet as strangers, stand as equals, share more in common than is visible on the surface.

Encounter carries potential for an appreciation of differences and reduction of barriers to connection. Strangers engage, share a moment, part in a friendly spirit. Or not.

A man sings nearby, guitar case open for money. Offered a poem in gratitude for his music, he retorts loudly: *I need money, not a damn poem.* Nothing to be done. As the instigator walks away, he continues yelling at no one in particular.

Who can tell when a bear will be unwittingly poked? It's a risk one takes.

In the wake of a single act, unseen ripples can move the heart. The instigator wonders to this day: where is he now?

Evolution

Novel forms of instigation, for instance, a poetry riot, may spring to life sometime in the future. Perhaps more instigators will take to the streets with poetry for the masses. All that's known for certain is that everything becomes apparent in due time.

September 2020: Sad But So Footnote

This entry was submitted for inclusion in the encyclopedia in January 2020. COVID-19 hit two months later. During shelter-in-place, the instigator went to an empty downtown Bend weekly, gave herself a poem, snapped a photo, and returned home. After Bend was back in business, the masked instigator resumed delivery to her business route. But handing out poems to strangers during a pandemic didn't seem wise. Thus, the heart of this spontaneous, spirited endeavor evaporated. For her last instigation on July 22, the instigator gave out absurd dream-poems she'd written, then called it a day for this social experiment. She continues to write and spread poetry in whatever ways she can. Instigation never ends.

~Krayna Castelbaum

"Headin' on over to Bend, Oregon.
Whole lotta shaking' going on in Bend!

—Gordon Cole. "Twin Peaks, Season 2 Quotes." *Quotes.net.* 1990. Accessed 1 Sep. 2020.

G

Glow: *verb:* to steadily incandesce

Trinity Episcopal Church

Only in deep winter does
red, green, and golden light
paint patterns on the priest
at noontime Eucharist
in the chapel.

These three
tall colored windows tell no tales
of apostolic life and martyrdom,
unlike those that decorate the nave
of the main church.

There,
above old wooden pews,
the glaziers framed stained symbols—
bread, ships and shells,
knives, keys, and crosses —
forgotten signs of death, delight
and travel from the lives of those
who thought they'd met the Sun.

But glass-emblems in the chapel
aren't so clear. What meanings
move through curls of color?
What can't a circle say?

So like the patterned rose over the altar,
these windows utter "only" color
and design, un-languaged beauty.

And each year as our planet
tilts us away from warmth
and our star grows distant
as deliverance sometimes seems,
these hues against the pastor's
ivory alb remind us
                              we are
each other's light and warmth,

                              and love
is rarely as distant as it seems.

                              ~Kake Huck

G

Grounds: *noun:* territory, land; a large enclosed, mostly
earthen area

Lots, vacant

crisscross of bike tracks
sagebrush
columbine
spitting of Oregon grape
worn-down juniper
those berries
the mule deer with the bum hip
wrapper for a fast-food chain

we have nowhere near here
three signs from last month's
                elections
the red ants
the dust

the
distant
Peaks

~Ben Paulus

H

Halcyon: *adjective:* peaceful, happy, associated with kingfisher in classical myth

Belted Kingfisher (Megaceryle alcyon)

I dip a long paddle into the Deschutes River as a male kingfisher wheels past on wings storming blue and white. Staccato calls rain down on the currents. I know he's a male by his bluish-gray, heart-shaped neck band upon a snowy white chest. Only the females proclaim the belt of cinnamony red, a rarity in the bird world where males tend to be the glamorous gender. A second male clamors from a willow branch. His navy blue crest tousles in the July breeze. Then, he's arrowing toward the first in mid-river. My paddleboard slips between them and for one elated moment I'm in the aerial dance.

Ranging across the fish-filled waters and coastlines of North America, the belted kingfisher is the only species found in Canada and the U.S., except near the southern border, where ringed and green kingfishers dwell. In central Oregon, the males tend to remain year round on ice-free waters, while females are more likely to fly south for the winter.

Kingfishers seek riffles for best fishing and guard their territories from rivals. They land on tree limbs and won't turn down a handy perch upon a wire strung across a river. Often skittish, they adapt to us, too. The local artist Andy Wachs who built the steel sculpture "Kingfisher" by Bend's Old Mill District (installed in 2016) created an abstract tree and practical perch that the birds favor. Nearby, at the Bend Whitewater Park, artist Sandy Klein painted a belted kingfisher within a wildlife mural above the Colorado Avenue pedestrian tunnel.

For a decade, I've lived under a kingfisher spell, ever since witnessing a pair raise a family on the banks of a forested creek in Montana. For the month of June, I had spent hours in a camouflaged blind, often flummoxed by the hard-to-pin down behaviors of birds that never once accepted my presence unless I remained invisible.

Recently, when paddling upstream from Dillon Falls on the Deschutes, I spotted an unusual nest in the deep soils of the root wad of a fallen pine. I'd noted the tennis ball-sized hole with twin furrow marks at the base etched by the feet of kingfishers entering and exiting. Typically, the birds dig horizontal tunnels that ascend slightly into vertical earthen streambanks. After excavating for several days with their tiny shovel toes (all kingfishers have one toe fused to another for better digging—a feature called syndactyly), the pair hollows out a football-sized burrow at the end of the tunnel that may extend four to even eight feet deep.

There, the female will lay seven eggs (usually)—one a day and only then will she warm them with her brood patch to assure synchronous hatching. Both parents take turns incubating. A month later, the featherless chicks will chip their way out of the pearly white eggs. The feeding frenzy begins as the parents deliver prey to the fast-growing juveniles. Darting in and out of the dirt hole with fish, the adult kingfishers perform yet another feat—they never seem to have a speck of dirt on their white breast feathers. To find and then observe an active nest is so challenging and the parents so fierce to intruders that few people witness the event.

This halcyon bird, forever linked to an ancient Greek myth of transformation and happiness, always cleaves the air with a sweet ratchet of notes. Always the kingfisher leads and vanishes around the next bend. Always the kingfisher invites the chase and the dream of becoming for one instant the bird of the headfirst dive, of slalom flight, of circling joy, of heart-stopping hover, and of rocketing speed so low to a river that wingtips flick whitewater droplets.

~Marina Richie

H

Hunger: *noun:* appetite, wish, desire

The Family Kitchen (Volunteer)

"to serve anyone who needs a nutritious meal in a safe
and caring environment."
—the mission statement of The Family Kitchen in
Bend, Oregon

For several months a family joined our
regulars: two kids with folks who
worked but didn't have the bucks
for first and last and cleaning.
They lived inside their car.
The little girl disliked when different
foods would touch. "It's ick," she said.
Our kitchen platers, rubber gloved,
would push her meat and veg to edge
as if to say, "You're safe and heard."

And so we try, we many volunteers,
to welcome all: the hurting
and the homeless, lost individuals
beside small groups of friends and
family, the "truly needy" and the fraud.

For even hungry cheats must eat.
Our job is not to judge. We work
to offer comfort, sustenance, security
and hope for all who enter here,
if only for an hour or two each day.
And though we sometimes grumble
over waste and comment on a crazed
or testy guest, I just remember
Matthew 25 – go read! And then
remember how our task is blessed.

So send your dollars now!
The website has a button to donate.
Don't wait to share your plenty
with a stranger. Come in!
Enjoy! We're saving you a plate.

~Kake Huck

"In comparison [to Portland],
Bend is about as cultural as a trout.
However, for a smallish community, [it] has a
surprising number of talented artists…"

—Mariah Wilson. "Bend Versus Portland." *The Bulletin.* 1 Sept.
2018. Updated 31 Jan. 2020. Accessed 1 Sept. 2020.

I

Instinct: *noun:* inner knowing, discernment, gut feeling

Migration Of the Monarchs, Eastern Cascades

NAME: Monarch Butterfly, Danaus Plexippus
DESCRIPTION: 3 inches long with rich, radiant cinna-mon-orange wings veined and outlined in black.

The monarch butterfly is the world's only major mi-grating butterfly and one rarely seen in northwestern Ore-gon, but it is common east of the Cascades in the summer as it prepares for its fall trip south to Mexico and coastal California.

NAME: Oregon Department of Corrections Saw Crew, Adultus Incustodexippus
DESCRIPTION: 6 foot, 3 inches with bright, visible hunter-orange coverings veined and outlined in soot.

We, the ten-man crew, are tasked with falling acres of wild-fire-scorched standing snags. Fall, limb, buck, stack; rinse and repeat. Located at the foot of the south Sister, on the east side of this magnificent mountain range, there have been several transformative wild fires. After the pyres we assembled are set ablaze, come the cold months, the Forestry Department will replant.

From chaos a renewing order is grown.

It may not be that hot, I've been hotter, but the greasy, sawdust covered, thirty five pound chainsaw puts cardio heart rates into perspective. There's still snow on the mountain peaks and the stiff gusts are about thirty degrees cooler than the ambient air.

Gasoline and bar oil crawls down my chaps, creating a tacky fly-trap for the powdered clay erupting around every boot step. The arid, dusty aroma; mingles alongside pungent diesel fumes, with young wild strawberry blooms, while the three-year-old soot from the standing snag looms.

It looms aloft, like a reminder of some bad choice. Akin to the looming, inside of prison housing; fetid, recycled, and stagnant. Mirroring the attitudes and behaviors of its occupants.

After four years, with nothing but the grey-noise-chatter of two-thousand perpetually entitled repining children, the silence out here can feel overwhelming.

The depths come upon us quickly, from horizon to trench. As we walk, our subconscious foot pulls us forward the direction that it chooses. Do you remember to point your toes, or do you just follow where they lead?

Off-the-chart decibels of the two-stroke tree-eaters finish their banshee wails through our crispy matchstick labyrinth. Now for an hour of fire-watch and machine maintenance.

With my petrol powered scythe, stripped down, cleaned out then put back together, in a puzzle-box of effort, it's time to sharpen. The bastard round file's scales bite into the undercut steel tooth of the saw's killing bits. Each push-and-twist erases the evidence of hostile rocks that silently saltated from the Earth and challenged it's keen consumption.

An hour just isn't enough, when you recall we have to go back. Suddenly, every moment wanes light speed.

So-I slow my breath, my mind, my senses. I absorb.

I am a sponge. Porous and neutral. Anticipating the release of pressure that signals a drawing in of stimuli.

The air now, is clean, a sampling taste of white and green; snow's repletant sheen, abundant verdure in-between.

The wind calms down-a parade begins.

Thousands of newly hatched Monarch butterflies break free of their cocoons and flutter on first used wings, to dance across the hilltops.

With the poise and grace of a prima ballerina, a fresh twice-born Sprite lands on the back of my hand. She is statuesque in her being, between my black-blood-scabbed knuckles and the tan line of grime left where my glove covered my wrist.

Her presence is gossamer. She has apparition, like an incontestable guide sharing secret mysteries. She is saturated with spontaneous intuition. Self-doubt, un-certainty, and guilt are characters she will never know.

Her strength-inherent knowledge, she shares willingly.

An infant scholar.

I pause, drinking her in as she whispers to me of Labors and Silken Cages, of Transmutation and Rebirth, of Migration and Instinct. Her message soaks through bone. I absorb her every utterance of passion and sovereignty.

I am bliss.

Endorphins waterfall from my cerebral cortex and hypothalamus, through my endocrine and limbic systems, migrating down my vertebrae, then out to every nerve ending about me.

A mist evaporates. Haze, like a rusted, barnacle-encrusted seaweed-festooned anchor, is cut away from the yoke of my mind.

On the porch of the portcullis is when I used to ponder, not whether to enter or recede, but to why I'm at the gateway. Should I seek an uncomfortable pathway, so that my voyage has more meaning?

I see so clearly now, that I am my own device.

A product, refined, pro-created from generations. Molded by the humanity of my Ancestor's choices.

Have you felt the pull? Never to pause too long at the crossroads, just knowing which way to step.

The abundance of hesitation is the mind's arguments trying to justify instinct.

"No need to stand on ceremony!" Keeps ringing in my head.

Progress is the lack of hesitation.

Shelter. Food. Sex. Sure, baser motivations drive us, but how often do you not rest when your body tells you it's exhausted? Not eat as your stomach moans to be sated? Well, the third one-you'll get no argument from me, lest passion precedes precedent.

The ease with which I stumble reaffirms that I've trusted my salt-blood; as when the tides roil from the guardianship of the Moon. Do as thou wilt, shall be the whole of Nature's Law.

Self-pity. Remorse. Regrets. I have none. Should I feel guilty on this? No, I think not. For without the folly of man, the Fool might not begin his journey. Or, worse yet-I may not find my bindle filled with wisdom and experience, when the dark and revered, immortally patient, chauffeur to the Underworld, pulls his last breath from my lungs and reclaims my bones to enrich the rooted soil of my kin.

She has whispered to me her secrets. The magic of intuition. She bound my skull in a chrysalis with ribbons of cinnamon-orange and charcoal-black.

My Nirvana, Equanimity and Humility - for Eternity.

~Angelo Di Nocenzo

#13658064
11 February 2020

J

Jaw: *noun:* bone of the mouth that enables biting and chewing; a seizing mechanism

Bones in Rake's Meadow

Fremont-Winema National Forest

I was practically inside the rib cage of a cow skeleton before I realized it was stretched before me, huge and horrible. Sedges and grasses had grown thick through the vertebrae and between the ribs, concealing the bones well. Now I could see the whole skeleton: stretched on its back, ribs curved up and around like barrel staves, one leg poised straight up as if the beast had died begging for a belly rub. The long neck twisted to the edge of snapping from the skull's weight, and two enormous jawbones opened to the sky.

Jack Creek had chunks of ice puzzle-pieced around the sedges that morning. The creek stayed cold, hunkered down in the long morning shadows. It seemed like the first morning ever in the meadow; the sun was eager and warm, and juncos burst back and forth between a downed log and some old pines. Two flickers skidded and foraged.

September is miserly with color in Rake's Meadow. There is green—the sedges and rushes and grasses. The pumice earth is a light, clean ochre, beautiful but merciless; not everything can grow in it. There are occasional flecks of lavender, the purple aster, and a much less occasional deep yellow, a monkeyflower down on the wet bank. Dead and downed trees, the ones that seem they will crack and burn as you stare, shimmer a gray-silver.

And the white bones. Cow, deer, and elk bones. Femurs, vertebrae, and skulls lay scattered, bleached and brilliant, looking out of place, forgotten. Later, I found a small half jawbone—fawn, or coyote. I felt its smooth scrubbed dove shape with my fingers, my palms. I thought about the fact that millions of years sculpted that jawbone, and that millions of jawbones lie around in meadows, under trees, at the bottoms of canyons and rivers. I wondered what it meant to love a place. Do we love a place for itself, or because we see parts of ourselves in it? *Rib, belly, burst. Miser, mercy, shimmer.* I looked at the broken bone, now terrible, now beautiful. I jiggled each tooth and put it in my pocket.

–Ellen Santasiero

J

John Day Fossil Beds National Monument: *noun:* a nationally-recognized place to see a geological record of 40 million years of plant, animal, climate, and ecosystem evolution

John Day Fossil Beds National Monument

John Day **Fossil** Beds contains one of the most complete Cenozoic stratigraphic sequences in the world. The **fossils** of the John Day Basin have been of interest to research for over 150 years beginning with Thomas Condon, O. C. Marsh, and E. D. Cope and later followed by J. C. Merriam, Ralph Chaney, and many others. It was clear that the vertebrate and plant records in the region were a valuable resource to the scientific community. J. C. Merriam was one of the early proponents of protecting the **fossil** beds as public land and by the 1930s, three state parks had been created; Thomas Condon-John Day **Fossil** Beds State Park, Clarno State Park, and Painted Hills State Park. The 14,000 acre monument was authorized when the enabling legislation adopted by Congress was signed into law on October 26, 1974 and was established in 1975. Additionally, the creation of the monument was supported by the Governor and Legislature of the State of Oregon (Senate Report 93-1233 1974). The monument consists of three separate and distant units that included lands that were previously protected by the State of Oregon, federal agencies, and private landowners. However, the Bureau of Land Management, Fish and Wildlife Service, Bureaus of Indian Affairs, Forest Service, and the State of Oregon manage several other important **fossil** sites within the John Day river valley not included in the Congressional boundaries but are still protected. The long history of collecting in the area has meant that **fossil** material can be found in many repositories across North America (Table 1). With 197 confirmed type specimens (Tweet, Santucci and McDonald 2016), a relatively continuous section, abundant plant and animal **fossils**, and numerous volcanic layers (e.g., ashes, ignimbrites, and lava flows), John Day **Fossil** Beds is a unique resource. The geologic layers at John Day **Fossil** Beds cover about forty million years of the Cenozoic, namely the Clarno, John Day, Mascall, and Rattlesnake formations (Fig. 1). The history of evolution and changing climates is well preserved within these public lands. The Eocene aged Clarno Formation (54-39 Ma) is about 1800 m thick and includes both volcanic and volcanogenic sedimentary rocks deposited by lava flows, ashfalls, lahars, and fluvial mechanisms (Bestland, Hammond, et al. 1999, Dillhoff, et al. 2009, McClaughry, et al. 2009). The

Hancock Mammal Quarry and the Clarno Nut beds are the most charismatic sites from the National Park Service administered Clarno Formation outcrops representing a diverse flora and fauna. Although excavations ended in the 1960s, new discoveries are being made on those same **fossils** 50 years later (Robson et al. 2019; Emery, Davis, and Hopkins 2016; Samuels and Korth 2017). The John Day Formation (39-18 Ma) is currently subdivided into seven members: Big Basin, Turtle Cove, Kimberly, Haystack Valley, Balm Creek, Johnson Canyon, and Rose Creek (Retallack, Bestland and Fremd 2000, Hunt and Stepleton 2004, Albright III, et al. 2008). There is a rich **fossil** record of plants and animals persevered as well as **fossil** soils, or paleosols. Thirteen of the volcanic layers in the John Day Formation are named and many of them have been radiometrically dated. One of the largest volcanic deposits is the Picture Gorge ignimbrite (28.7 Ma) in the Turtle Cove Member which was a large caldera eruption possibly associated with the Yellowstone Hotspot (Seligman, et al. 2014). The John Day Formation includes some rare and interesting taxa including one of the last North American Primates before the arrival of Humans, Ekgmowechashala zancanellai (Samuels, Albright, and Fremd 2015). Mascall Formation (~17-13 Ma) is composed of volcaniclastic sediment derived from the coeval volcanoes of Oregon, Washington, and Nevada (Rytuba and McKee 1984, Bestland, Forbes, et al. 2008). Like the John Day Formation, there are several paleosols preserved. A well preserved floral assemblage (leaves and pollen) can be found in the lower diatomite layers and there is a good record of extinct vertebrates throughout the entire Mascall Formation (Chaney 1959, Downs 1956). The Rattlesnake Formation (~ 7 Ma) is the stratigraphically highest geologic unit and is composed of fluvial deposits (Enlows 1976, J. E. Martin 1983, Martin and Fremd 2001) and is dissected by the Rattlesnake Ash Flow Tuff (7.05 Ma). Plant **fossils** are rare in the Rattlesnake Formations (Dillhoff, et al. 2009), but there are numerous vertebrate **fossils** that were first described in 1925 and include the first occurrence of true beavers and fishers (Merriam, Stock and Moody 1925, Samuels and Zancanella 2011, Samuels and Cavin 2013). One fascinating story that is persevered at John Day **Fossils** Beds is the evolution of the horse. **Fossils** of 24 species of horse can be found through the entire section which chronical this family's evolution in the face of an environment changing from a closed forest to an open grassland (Fremd 2010).

~Nicholas A. Famoso

"When I lived in Oregon …
I couldn't handle the scale of the West;
the mountains were just too massive, too
powerful. They were only for the wanderings
of the gods, not for human me."

—Gayle Pemberton. *The Hottest Water in Chicago.* Wesleyan University Press, 1998.

K

Keep: *noun:* the strongest and securest part of a medieval fortress

The Castle

The Oregon Badlands was declared a National Wilderness Area by Congress in 2009. The Badlands is home to a variety of desert-dwelling fauna, stunning wildflowers, and ancient junipers. Visitors can explore the unique rock formations formed by the area's main lava flow, and possibly find traces of human history.

Long ago, in the time of large animals, humans were small and weak and soft and took shelter wherever they could: in trees, under trees, in shallow depressions in the ground, and so on. They were regularly eaten.

They prayed to the earth to give them shelter and protection, until finally, one day, the earth sent up rings of molten rock. When they cooled, the humans ventured inside. They found pairs of walls surrounding an opening in the middle.

One of these they called The Castle. Which was quite a coincidence as they had never seen a castle; it was just a word they made up (like sponge), but they like the hard consonant K followed by the tinkling STL sound.

And then it rained and rained, and the opening in the middle of The Castle filled with water and became a lake, which attracted a friendly dragon who used its fiery breath to heat up the water so it was really nice to sit in on cool evenings with a cocktail and look up at the stars. The large animals tried to get inside the walls to eat the humans, but the humans threw rocks at them and called them names and the dragon spewed fire to scare them away, occasionally igniting a random juniper tree.

The standoff between the animals and the humans got boring—the animals couldn't get in to eat the humans, and the humans grew weary of so much safety—so they eventually tamed the beasts, invented the wheel, and left for the coast.

The lake dried up, but the dragon awaited the humans' return. After many years, it died of loneliness.

If you go: Park at the Flatiron Rock Trailhead near mile marker 16 on Highway 20 and follow one of two trails (Flatiron Rock or Ancient Juniper) to Flatiron Rock (look for burnt juniper trees on your way!), then take a right on the Castle Trail. Once inside The Castle, make your way into the middle where the lake once was and kick around in the pumice, you may find dragon scales.

~Mike Cooper

K

Know-how: *noun:* ability to do a specific thing

What to Know about the Oregon Desert Trail

The Oregon Desert Trail isn't a trail.

You will see more pronghorn antelope than people.

It's really more of a virtual route.

Route means 750-miles consisting of 10% trail, 35% cross-country travel and 55% roads (primarily old two-track dirt roads) and virtual means no signage. Extreme!

On a scale from 1-10 of difficulty (1 being the Deschutes River Trail and 5 being the Pacific Crest Trail), the Oregon Desert Trail is an 11.

The route looks like a big "W" through southeastern Oregon.

It starts just outside Bend in the Badlands Wilderness (ancient juniper trees!) then heads south near Summer Lake (hot springs!) to almost touch California near Lakeview (Oregon's tallest town!), winding northeast again to meet Steens Mountain (glaciated canyons!), south to the Nevada border near Denio (hot, hot, hot!), up through the Oregon Canyon Mountains (views!), down again to McDermitt, Nevada (Nevada again?), and then through Oregon's grand canyon in the Owyhee River (swimming and slot canyons!) to end at Lake Owyhee State Park near the Idaho border (whew.).

Less than 30 people have hiked all 750 miles of the route.

There are lots of hot springs to soak away the misery of bushwhacking through thick sagebrush.

You can visit Old Perpetual, a geyser near Lakeview.

Cheryl Strayed finished writing "Wild" in the small town of Plush.

LOTS of petroglyphs and arrowheads can be found throughout the desert.

You can visit a public collection area for the Oregon Sunstone in the Warner Valley.

Evidence of the OLDEST Native Americans in the country is along the route: over 14,000 years old. (that's old!)

The only (that I know of) "trail" to be created by a conservation organization: Oregon Natural Desert Association.

The route's mission is: to engage the recreation community in the conservation of eastern Oregon.

Fields, Oregon has amazing milkshakes.

There are a lot of cows out there.

The sky is some of the darkest in the country (star gazing!)

A dry lakebed near the route has mammoth tracks dating over 43,000 years ago.

Better channel your inner camel; some reliable water stretches are 40 miles apart.

It passes through the Steens Mountain Wilderness, the only cow-free wilderness in the country.

Steens Mountain is considered one mountain, at 50-miles long.

Sometimes you need to drink out of dirt cow ponds (including poo too), so bring a GOOD water filter and a strong stomach.

When in the Malheur National Wildlife Refuge, look for birds: it supports anywhere between 5 and 66 % of the Pacific Flyway's migrating populations for priority waterfowl.

The Owyhee Canyonlands was formed (15 million years ago that is) by the super volcano hotspot that currently sits under Yellowstone National Park.

All of this area is part of the Great Basin.

The trail follows part of the 30-mile Abert Rim, one of the highest fault scarps in the country (almost 2,500' above the valley below!).

It will hurt so good.

~Renee Patrick

L

Lava Dome: *noun:* a rounded protrusion of earth out of which molten rock once flowed

Pilot Butte

Pilot Butte is a lava dome that swells like a pregnant belly. In other words, a cinder cone. In other words, a volcano. Maybe six months along. Pilot Butte is a lava dome that lifts upward from the town of Bend, Oregon, the back of a hand extending from town to sky, waiting for a kiss of genuflection. It sits at over 4,000 feet above sea level and rises 500 feet above its surroundings. It is high enough, but not too high.

From below, it is a marker, a rounded reference point on the east side of Bend. East of the parkway, east of the river. From the top, you can see even further east – past Costco and Whole Foods and homes laid out on grids, past ranchettes and small farms and the city airport, past the Badlands and beyond. If you wanted to, you could face north. You could walk to the other side of the butte and face south, then west. If you wanted to, you could trace a circle on the rim of Pilot Butte with your feet. Or spiral up the path from bottom to top, as if entering into a Fibonacci sequence. From this vantage point—at the top of Pilot Butte on its western side—you can see several peaks of the Cascade Range, peaks with names like South Sister, Broken Top, and Bachelor, peaks trimmed with snow in the middle of summer.

Once, in winter, I unloose myself into the early morning dark with snowshoes strapped to my feet. It doesn't always snow in town, but this time it has. The butte is covered in soft washes of white that glow pink before dawn. Any sharp edges have wafted away; sound is muffled alongside smell, taste. The metallic dust of the high desert scrubland steppe—pungent and molecular—is gone. Everything has turned to water. I pick up a handful of water and form it into a ball. I let the ball be flung from my hand only to watch it break against a juniper trunk. I throw another and then I keep walking. I reach the top before sunrise and watch as, yet again, a town is born into light.

Some people try to walk the butte every day. Some people have walked it over a hundred times. Some people sprint the mile to the top in an annual foot race put on by a local running club.

It is no small thing: to, one moment, be amidst the sage-and bitterbrush and the next be above them as if on a perch or in a high nest. What are we made of if not this eagle eye view?

Once upon a time, 4th of July fireworks were launched over Mirror Pond in Bend. Nowadays they are shot from the top of Pilot Butte, year after year setting off fire after fire below the peonies or chrysanthemums, willows or diadems sparking up the sky. The Fire Department is always on hand and the fires are always put out quickly. Still, what does this say? To bring a flame into a tinder-box knowing there will be consequences.

~Brigitte Lewis

L

Local Eats: *noun:* produce or other food grown, processed, or cooked in one's home region

A letter from central Oregon to friends in California

Greetings from central Oregon, the ancestral and current home of the Warm Springs, Wasco, and Northern Paiute People, where the ancient volcanoes of the Cascades meet the high desert sagebrush steppe and the Deschutes River makes its way to the mighty Columbia. I'm one of many new residents here.

I moved to Bend in 2019 to work for the High Desert Food and Farm Alliance, an organization that brings folks together to strengthen the food system, build community, and educate people about the gifts our land and its stewards can offer us. Since my arrival, I've noticed that many of the things I learned as a small farmer in California apply here, too. Even though the elevation is a bit lower, and the climate a bit drier, the soil sandier, and some cities bigger, small farmers here in central Oregon have the same challenges and opportunities as rural farmers in California.

Local food is always rooted in community. As in California, most farms here are family-run and usually multi-generational. In central Oregon, an amazing force of volunteers support farmers by showing up for a day to work, harvest, glean, or pack. There are groups like WWOLF (Willing Workers On Local Farms), The Edible Adventure Crew, and the Glean Team who bring farmers and eaters together and build understanding about what it takes to put food on plates. There's a farmers' market within a few miles of almost every city here, which is pretty impressive since central Oregon is mostly rural. In Bend, there is a whole store dedicated to local products - Central Oregon Locavore - which is open year-round and is a center for local food activity. A lot of other stores are working hard to supply local goods too, and so are many restaurants. The small farmers here strive to practice sustainable, regenerative farming and ranching so they will be able to feed the community far into the future.

We know that geographic distance can affect the quality, price, and availability of our food. In the winter of 2019, a big snowstorm closed the passes from the Willamette Valley. Within a day or so many store shelves were almost bare – it was a little shocking how quickly that happened. But when our local food systems are strong, we're all more secure in every way. In my job at HDFFA, I see local farmers play a huge part in making sure families experiencing hunger or food insecurity have healthy food to eat – in 2018, over 18,000 pounds of produce was donated by small farmers (and big gardeners) to central Oregon food banks, shelters, families, and individuals. The people who grow the spinach you buy in a plastic box from a big store just can't contribute to our communities like that, even though they might like to.

Folks here did an Economic Impact Study a few years back in 2016, and found that when people spend money on food coming from outside central Oregon, about 28 cents of every dollar stays in the community. When they spend that same dollar on locally grown, raised, or processed food, about 76 cents stays here – almost three times as much. No matter where you are, when you buy locally you are supporting not just farmers, but local distributors, retailers, restaurants, farm supply and equipment businesses, and your money is spent locally over and over again. This is a message local food advocates want to make sure everyone hears: your food dollars are guaranteed to be way more powerful when you spend them locally.

In central Oregon, when people buy locally from a store, visit the farmers market, patronize local businesses who offer local products, grow their own food, share their harvest and what they know, or contribute money or time to organizations like HDFFA, they help everyone in the community live a good life in this beautiful place we call home.

-Laurie Wayne

"[I hope my great grandchildren]
learn every aspect of tribal history
and their genealogy. I hope they take
an inordinate interest in that."

—George Aguilar. Warm Springs resident. "Ana-ku iwacha mi-mi."
High Desert Journal, 2005.

M

Massive: *adjective:* large; extraordinary in size or area

Skyline Forest

From a petroglyph that looks oh-so-phony but is certified authentic, to groves of third and fourth growth pines, remnants of once vibrant timber mills, canals that provided those mills with power, bits and pieces of a mill serving a narrow-gauge railway bed, and swaths of forest fire devastation, the Skyline Forest is a reminder of central Oregon's pre and not-too-distant history.

Stretching from north and west from Shevlin Park to Sisters, the forest is also home to elusive coyote, deer, elk, wild turkeys, badgers, and cougars that frequent the waters of Bull and Snag Springs at night.

For the outdoor recreation minded, Skyline offers miles of motorcycle created trails now shared with mountain bikers, hikers, and dog walkers plus miles of old logging roads for gravel grinding cyclists.

Yet for all it has to offer, the forest remains crowd free. In three years of 100 days per year mountain bike riding in the forest, my friend Terry Foley and I saw maybe 36 people.

However, we did witness two bull elk leading 40 cows down a trail one morning. Stunning, and just ten minutes from Bend's city limits.

~Bob Woodward

M

Meet: *noun:* a large gathering of athletes for competition

[Bend] Open Swim Meet @ Juniper Swim & Fitness Center: an annual competitive swimming competition held in August and hosted by Bend Swim Club and JSFC, where camping is permitted on the grounds of Juniper Park, located on the eastside of Bend, Oregon, for participating swimmers and their families.

[Bend] Open Swim Meet @ Juniper Swim & Fitness Center

One of the great selling points of the house we bought on the eastside of Hwy 97 in Bend in 1999, after renting an apartment on a charming cul de sac on the pedestrian-friendly westside (besides its there must be something wrong with it price) was its proximity to Juniper Park and the JSFC—a jewel of a civic facility set amid a residential forest of, yes, juniper trees, with both indoor and outdoor pools, where my daughters and I spent much of their K-5 extra-curricular hours, and every day in summer, except for one weekend in hottest August, when Bend Swim Club hosts the Bend Open Swim Meet, and the rolling greenery is dotted with yellow and red nylon tents, camp chairs, propane stoves, and makeshift clotheslines dripping with Speedo and TYR racing suits.

In many ways it felt like a takeover. One year a local boy, about twelve or thirteen, stationed himself in a ponderosa among the raven nests to keep an eye on things. My husband referred to him as Park Boy, a superhero-style defender of residential integrity, but I am still unclear on the boy's motivation. We took it for granted he lived adjacent to or near the park, and thereby felt some level of protectiveness of his turf, but who wouldn't be dazzled by, and want a front seat to, all that glistening athleticism, let alone the compelling carnival of community presented by this yearly pop-up event?

During the school year, a steady parade of Chevy Suburbans, Honda Pilots, and Land Rover Range Rovers emitted children at the entrance of the pool for swim practice or lessons. Really dedicated young swimmers joined the JSFC League or Bend Swim Club, slides on their feet even in winter, a signature ratty towel hung round their wet napes as they folded themselves back into the SUV, with its Bend Swim Club sticker on the back windshield, headed to homework and dinner. The Open, when it came around, was just that—open—drawing freestylers, backstrokers, breaststrokers, and butterflyers from all over the State, plus parts of Washington and California, in addition to the local, eligible talent.

The daughters and I would inevitably rim the perimeter of the park on meet days, the pool closed to us, every year surprised by the occupation. We observed lanky adolescents rooting around in coolers, goggles bouncing on clavicles, little brothers and sisters snaking around their neighbors' campsites, one of them pulled by an alien dog on a leash. Swim moms swarmed in groups facing the 50-meter outdoor pool, humming about schedules, heats, sipping from huge travel cups, handing out fruit leather and chips, with another, much smaller dog peeking out from a tote or pertly watching the action from a lap.

I am past my irritation at being inconvenienced in the height of summer, and have moved on to a feeling of nostalgia, even as I anticipate this year's Open and the pool's public closure, no longer so critical now that the daughters are women. I am experiencing a feeling of loss for something that yet exists, but which feels precarious—a tent pitched among many for a summer weekend in a residential park, hot dogs and cold cuts sandwiches, dollar store games for the little ones, young people slipping away for parking lot conversations between heats, and, in flip flops and hoodies, circling the wooded path and each other around the park as the sun sets.

My husband reminded me of Park Boy. I'd forgotten him, and his watch. It occurs to me now that he may have taken up his post at other times, too, not just during the Open. I wonder if he had a pool pass, if he'd ever been to the pool at his park at all, where he lives now.

~Irene Cooper

N

Native: *adjective:* found in nature, indigenous

Crooked River Wetlands Complex

On days when I work in Prineville, it's a delight to take my lunch break at the Crooked River Wetlands Complex. On any given day I might see young parents pushing a baby in a stroller with a toddler on a kiddie bike, a couple exercise-walking on the paved trails, or people with binoculars or cameras aimed at birds of all sorts in and around the wetlands. Every day there is different, but one day stands out in my mind.

Perched on a roadside post, the bird looked left, then right, lingering, as if to allow this amateur birder sufficient time to memorize its features for later identification. The brilliant yellow hue of its head and chest stood in stark contrast to the ink black of its body. Only when it finally took flight did I notice a small white stripe on the wing. Entranced by the bird's beauty, I paused after it had flown away, savoring the moment. Later, I learned that I had seen a male Yellow-headed Blackbird. Not uncommon in the Wetlands Complex—in fact, it was "Bird of the Month in April 2019"—but it was a first for me.

The Crooked River Wetlands Complex, just two miles west of Prineville on the Lone Pine/O'Neil Highway, opened in April of 2017. It is situated along the Crooked River as it flows westward toward Lake Billy Chinook. Encompassing 120 acres, the Wetlands Complex was designed to increase wastewater capacity for the city of Prineville. But, above and beyond this benefit, the Complex has extensive recreational, educational, and environmental values.

Imagine this: fifteen ponds with abundant vegetation and water. Over 200 different birds and water fowl. Five miles of trails for walking, hiking, biking, dogs on leash. More than a dozen educational kiosks. Kids In Parks adventures for children and families. Monarch wayside station and pollinator garden. Eagle Scout projects and school children involvement. Covered picnic shelter with adjoining restrooms.

According to the city of Prineville's website, people have seen numerous other birds over the past couple of years. The web site features photos of 16 unusual bird sightings—birds that are not typically seen in this area. Another photo gallery shows pictures of more commonly seen birds, and I have my own personal list of birds and waterfowl that I hope to see there one day.

At the top of my list is the Western Meadowlark, the state bird of Oregon. Also on my list are the Cinnamon Teal, the Yellow Warbler, the Mountain Bluebird, and the American Kestrel. Not that I don't want to see any others, but these are of particular interest to me.

If you, like me, enjoy seeing birds in the wild, or just like to hike, picnic, or enjoy a bit of nature along a desert river, I encourage you to take a trip to the Crooked River Wetlands Complex!

~Leila A. Shepherd

"John A. Brown was the first African-American
homesteader in central Oregon,
without question. He was one of the first
homesteaders in this area of any race."

—Jarold Ramsey, Madras resident. *An Oregon Canyon*. Donnell Alexander and Sika Stanton, 2017.

O

Original: *adjective:* independent and creative in thought or action

Sparrow Bakery: beloved Bend bakery with a cult-like following. Home of the Ocean Roll, a spiral-shaped pastry consisting of croissant dough hand-rolled in a paste of sugar, fresh ground cardamom, and vanilla extract.

Sparrow Bakery's Ocean Roll has a cult-like following. The pastry is a hallowed tradition of Christmas mornings. It's been stacked three stories tall to form wedding cakes and shipped overnight for birthday celebrations. "People's opinion of the Ocean Roll is my litmus test," says Liz Skarvelis, a yoga teacher from Redmond. "If I love you, you're probably getting an Ocean Roll with a candle stuck in it for your birthday." When Snoop Dogg toured through Bend, the local newspaper published a cartoon imagining the rapper ate the iconic pastry while visiting, and decided to become a permanent resident.

The Ocean Roll origin story begins—fittingly—at the Oregon Coast. Sparrow co-founders Whitney Keatman and Micah Jordan were dreaming up a menu when struck by the unexpected use of cardamom in the cinnamon roll at Bread and Ocean in Manzanita. The pair swapped the traditional brioche base of a cinnamon roll with their croissant dough—"we knew we had a really good croissant recipe," says Keatman—and transported a reincarnation of the roll's sugary glaze into the spiraled folds.

Sparrow opened in a 650-square foot space in the Old Ironworks District in 2006, and has grown by leaps and bounds since. A second retail location opened in the Northwest Crossing neighborhood in 2014, followed by a 3,300 square foot production facility five years later to meet growing demand for breads and sweet treats from grocery stores and local restaurants. On a midsummer Saturday this year, Sparrow sold over 600 Ocean Rolls, and expects to double that number on Christmas Eve.

Ocean Roll dough is hand-folded, a rare practice among commercial bakers. A machine called a sheeter is more traditionally used to flatten the dough to a desired thickness. Keatman and Jordan were boot-strapping when they opened and didn't have cash for a sheeter. Over time, as the bakery's fame rose, and purchasing a sheeter became possible, the conscious choice was made to continue hand rolling. The shift would have altered their showcase product, making the dough flakier and less dense. "We strive to be something both original and timeless with everything we do."

~Sarah Cyr

P

Placed: *adjective:* to be put in a particular state

Now It Seems

for Natalie

So I have a friend
in every city now it seems.

Now it seems like I'll be thirty-two
with dandelions still ringing in my ears.

Funny:
    today I found a crack in the mirror:
    a crow's foot running from my eye,
    and I learned that I am weathered now—
    that I have waited out
    some terrible storm of interims,
and now my voice comes quelled
through a wall of scar & gauze.

I really must tell you how easily
I go into dreams
in which I passionately tell strangers
about my dreams.
     I wake up
     and no one believes
that I have asked my mind's version of a dead friend
what it was like out there and all he said was
wake up Alex get out of my head.

Now it seems
a far-flung dawn lies heavy
with a searing ray of candor:

Friends, I have nothing to say.
I miss you and feel I will always miss you.

Your voices:
     the sound of so much blank paper
     lost & lovely
     in the wind…

The juniper on the nearby mountains:
still green, my friends.
Forever will be.

Summer careens into fall.

I am watching whitetail deer
through a chain-link fence
and two Blackfeet chant in loops
for the sky-medicine.

   I will be home in three years

and the first thing I'm going to do
is close my eyes & look at the sun.

                                    ~Alex Tretbar

P

Public Art: *noun:* works of skill and creativity exposed to general view

The Galveston-14th Street Roundabout

One of the first things I noticed about Bend, Oregon, when I moved here: all the traffic roundabouts. When I remarked on them, my brother, who was visiting from the state of Washington and is a veritable encyclopedia, said, "They decrease t-boning by 78%." I often wonder from whence he pulls statistics on command. I couldn't find out if he was correct, but I did find out that roundabouts—RABs, for short—have been "proven to safely decrease traffic delays and congestion." This is from the City of Bend's website. I'd googled: "How many traffic roundabouts are there in the city of Bend OR?" "About 30." That's the answer. Also, you will find a video about how to use them, a General Use Brochure, a Bicyclist Roundabout Brochure, a Child Activity Book, an Activity Book Answer Sheet for teachers, and a link to FAQs, including "What do we do about people who will not yield?" and "Do I get a turn to go?"

I picked the Galveston/14th Street RAB because I loved the bright orange, sheet metal sculpture in the middle of it. When I told Irene Cooper this—she is a near-native, having lived here for 23 years—she said, "Oh. The flaming-chicken?" (See citations on the Bend Open Swim Meet at Juniper Park and the Pandora moth hatch at Vince Genna Stadium in this encyclopedia for her entries.) Yes, I loved the flaming chicken. Partly because it was an unforgettable landmark that pointed the way downtown in a place where all the buildings and trees looked the same to me.

Just FYI, downtown is all of two streets, Wall and Bond, and about 5 blocks long but has many local restaurants and shops and a farmer's market on Wednesdays in summer and a green park along the river with benches where you can sit and gaze at the expensive homes across the way and watch the geese that poop everywhere. Once, evidently, the city killed them and fed them to the homeless, although the subsequent out-cry made that a one-time event. Such is local lore.

The flaming chicken, created by Frank Boyden in 2002, is actually called "Phoenix Rising" and is one of the first of 23 sculptures featured in the local 30 RABs. If you google "sculptures in roundabouts in Bend Or," you will find a site called "Roundabout Art Route," which features a picture of and information about each sculpture as well as a mapped route for viewing them. You can even vote for your faves. The flaming chicken rotates and because, as I drive the roundabout, I am watching for cars and bicyclists and pedestrians, since there are heavy fines for failing to yield, let alone for hitting someone, I didn't actually realize it was a fowl of any sort. I just saw bright orange sheet metal and it reminded me of a much larger sculpture, "Sonora" by David Black, in front of the library in downtown Tucson, Arizona. Like the flaming chicken, "Sonora" was the subject of much controversy and now that I google it, I see it's actually red. Sometimes just the whisper of resemblance will make you feel at home. Or homesick.

The Galveston Roundabout is also the site of Taco Salsa, which has, hands down, the best breakfast burritos I've ever eaten. We always order the bacon, egg, and potato burrito and the carne machaca and egg burrito, although we ask them to add beans to the machaca. Machaca is another way to say carne seca or dried meat; theirs is delicious, beef that's been roasted then dried and shredded and recooked with tomatoes, onions, and chiles. And their beans are some of the best ever. Creamy with lard, I'm sure. You can spend much more for breakfast at The Victorian, which is kitty corner from Taco Salsa, in a charming old red house. Outside, they have a fire pit with seats around it so that even on snowy days, one doesn't mind waiting for a table. There's also an outside bar where you can get the best Bloody Mary in Bend, or so they boast, a mimosa made with their signature champagne, hot chocolate, spiked or not, and, of course, coffee. Once you make it inside, there's an extensive menu, mostly variations on eggs benedict. The Victorian has been voted Best Bend Breakfast 15 times in its 30 years of existence.

Another restaurant on the Galveston Roundabout is the Parrilla Grill where I have never eaten but which is reputed to have the best fish tacos in town. Of course, my daughter and I actually make the best fish tacos in town: my son-in-law is a commercial fisherman in Alaska who brings us salmon and halibut that is wild-caught and flash-frozen on the boat. Plus we make amazing mango salsa and slaw and black beans. In short, our fish tacos are to die-for.

Besides, if I'm going out for Mexican, I want Taco Salsa, where the people in the kitchen are calling back and forth in Spanish, the booths, shiny vinyl, and the music, Mexican. Home away from home that makes the Galveston Roundabout and, by extension, Bend, feel a little more like home.

~Beth Alvarado

"'I like to feel the ground,' Rock said.
'I like to stay here in one place and not move.'
Sagebrush said he felt the same way.'"

—Paiute story. "How the Animals Found Their Places. *Coyote was Going There: Indian Literature of the Oregon Country.* ed. Jarold Ramsey. University of Washington Press, 1980.

Question: *verb:* to interrogate

Breathing at Sea Level

The smell of greasy cheeseburgers filled the room as I worked my long shift at the Sisters Sno Cap Drive-in on a busy Sunday afternoon. That burger joint might as well have been my second home with the amount of hours I spent there. Groups of people began to line up.

"Good afternoon! How are you?" I asked a middle-aged woman, who had obviously waited a few too many minutes.

"I'll have a bacon cheeseburger with fries and a large Pepsi," she said.

"OK," I said, wondering why no one can return the greeting, but quickly brushed it off. "Would you like onions on your burger?"

"Yes, please. If you don't mind me asking, what are you?" she asked. That question every mixed or person of color dreads. The question to which you want to respond, "I'm a human, what about you?!" but I worked in the food industry where sarcasm towards customers was frowned on.

"I'm half black and half white." I forced a smile across my face.

"Really?! I never would've guessed! I thought you were Native American!" she said. I moved on to take an order from another customer.

That interaction wasn't the only time in central Oregon I'd been asked that question, a question that was not only impolite, but one that could also be crushing to one's identity.

My identity took a bit for me to be comfortable with. I was ultimately raised by my white family in Sisters, in a state with a deep history of racism. When I was younger, I struggled with acknowledging my African-American side because of my limited exposure to the African-American community, and a therapist suggested that that may have been the cause of some of my childhood anxiety.

At Sisters Elementary, other students recognized that I was different, but I never told anyone I was half black. I didn't feel comfortable with it and I didn't believe having that as part of my identity was important. Kids would always ask, "what's wrong with your hair?" to which I'd answer, *that's just how it is.* I began chemically straightening my hair, and continued to do so for 11 years because I wanted to fit in.

Three years after that interaction at Sno Cap, I had a conversation at Thump Coffee in downtown Bend with a local musician and artist who is also biracial. He did some of his growing up in Bend, and he said that due to his lack of experience with other African-Americans, he gets excited when he sees another black guy. "I want to ask my black questions from my black mind," he explained, while also being aware that people are more than just their skin tone. We talked about the history of racism, how to divide our identity into multiple parts, and why some African-Americans are less accepting of African-Americans with lighter skin tones.

Talking to this man about being biracial in central Oregon and openly discussing our respective identity crises felt like what I call "breathing at sea level." I wonder what it would be like to breathe at sea level all the time? To have open discussions with others who are struggling in similar ways? And not just one-on-one conversations, but a worldwide conversation that helps us accept each other through understanding each others' struggles? It's taken me years to claim half my identity, and I still deal with microaggressions, but it's part of who I am and I wouldn't change it for the world. It may be wishful thinking to think that racism will completely fade, but the least I can do is be open about who I am and how I feel.

Breathing at sea level feels like being in a nice coffee shop filled with people who converse and normalize and validate each other's feelings and findings about their identities, the smell of dark-roasted coffee drenching the air.

~Kennedy Lovette

R

Range: *noun:* the region throughout which a kind of organism or ecological community naturally lives or occurs

OPEN RANGE LOOSE STOCK

1. Loose stock in an open range
sage brush tall grass
we move on gravel roads
along a rolling horizon
where content livestock graze:
sheep, cows, bison, goats

Cottonwood Ryegrass
Wheeler 207, county
green river, tawny
running

and herds:
deer, antelope, elk
gravel tans and dusty dry grass
high desert subtle cracks of life
ochre green, yellow, dark brown and blue
juniper, ivory yellow patches and bone

2. A calm desolate longing
here, the ghosts of erased histories
and nomadic, listless solitude

At the center of town, a diner
I know places like this from my childhood
small towns in Minnesota, Wisconsin, Oklahoma
weak coffee, the color of the river

gravel roads extend from the diner
in a starpoint pattern to
ranchland, wilderness
those born here, young
sit at the diner counter
ordering greasy hash browns and eggs
those going to die here
clutch their pen, crossword in one hand
bottomless coffee mug in the other

and those, absent

~Alex Borgen

R

Rare: *adjective:* seldom occurring or found; marked by unusual quality

Botrychium pumicola, commonly known as the pumice moonwort, is a small, primitive, fern-related perennial rare plant that is restricted to the pumice-laden volcanic soils of central Oregon (with one outlier on Mt. Shasta). In its prime it is sea-green and leathery and graces us with its appearance for about two months in the summer. For the remainder of the year it resides quietly below ground, communing with its fungal partners and storing up reserves for its next appearance. Its populations are currently in decline in some areas where this narrative is set.

The footnotes for the following piece appear in the Appendix.

Pumice Moonwort

July 12, 1858. At RWE[1]'s urging that my health could be improved by a journey west to take the healing air,

I am here thus with Gray[2], in Oregon Territory, making collections for his taxonomic work. We have entered a forested undulating plain after leaving the sagebrush and grasses behind us to the east. Our peregrinations have taken us into a humble evergreen forest of pines we have been told make excellent subjects for teepee poles, due to their narrow girth and lack of a taper[3]. They are related to the pitch pines from home but contain 2 leaves per fascicle instead of 3, and the leaves are somewhat shorter. We can see white mountains some miles distant, further west, when we ascend one of the small rises in this modest countryside about us. We cannot linger more than an overnight here as there is no water to be encountered until some miles in a westerly direction where we are told a river flows.

Our rambles through this open, sunny forest have introduced us to soils bizarrely speckled with tan-colored pumice stones that lie atop a sandy subtext, presumably of high porosity. The stones are said to float, although we dare not use our water reserves to test it. These are prominently featured in variously-sized openings in this forest. The intense near-whiteness of these soils strain the eyes when encountered in the full sun.

Gray is familiar with some of the herbaceous species we have seen today from his knowledge of Hooker's[4] collections, although none are especially abundant here. Their paucity conveys a sense of nature's careful water budget. Those that do occur offer the traveler a welcome, striking smorgasbord of the yellows and whites of composites and purples and blues of penstemons and lupines against the pale soil.

We see an odd species that reminds me of the swamp moonwort I have seen in the meadows surrounding Concord. It is not that moonwort. Gray knows moonworts but not this one. It grows within the parched openings in the forest and is thickened and diminutive in disposition, as Gray tells me all moonworts he knows are wont to be, and as evidence cites the same unmistakable growth habit of sterile blade and separate stem bearing the spore packets looking much like diminutive clusters of grapes. Most of those we have seen today are fully sporulating, with tiny brown puffs let loose when the fertile frond is nudged with a finger.

We excavated several of these moonworts today and will carefully pack them so they will survive the trip home; Gray is especially eager to study them in comparison to the specimens extant in his herbarium. He feels strongly this is a species new to science.

The landscape does not offer expansiveness of view nor diversity of vegetation, yet serves to remind us the universe does not conform to one set of rules. The earth can say moonworts instead of oaks and still offer new delights to the observant traveler[5].

~Charmane Powers

"The more we know about a place,
the more we love it. The more we love it,
the more we take care of it."

—Anonymous

S

Stewardship: *noun*: the careful and responsible management of something entrusted to one's care

Stewardship

The face of central Oregon has been changing dramatically since the 1800s—first with the arrival of non-indigenous trappers such as Peter Skene Ogden, followed in turn by military and railroad explorers, homesteaders, irrigation entrepreneurs, farmers, land developers, and today, all of us. Over that time, native peoples suffered repeated deadly epidemics and dislocation, beaver and other animals were nearly or completely wiped out, cattle and sheep grazed from high desert to high mountains spread invasive weeds, over-zealous wildfire suppression led to unnaturally dense pine and juniper forests, and diversion of water through canals from above Bend to as far as Madras bled the Deschutes. In short, this eden was severely disrupted.

Through numerous boom and bust cycles, the pace of growth has steadily increased, today again reaching a fevered pitch in the decade following the 2008 Great Recession. Seemingly overnight, subdivisions and hotels are again popping up everywhere, traffic is on everyone's mind, and parking lots for many once-quiet trails are often overflowing. For many long-timers, the magic, tight-knit, small town days of Bend are over, but for most newcomers everything looks great compared to the places they fled. I'd posit that both are true, but what of our next future? As ever, it is in all of our hands to create. And if we are to succeed we must all play a positive part and not simply consume and exploit Bend's remaining character.

Despite the dramatic damage to this place, we do have a long history of citizens who've stepped up to protect and restore the landscapes and values that attracted so many of us to central Oregon. Signature early events to push back against indiscriminate development include the 1893 establishment of the Cascade Range Forest Reserve and the 1921 Women's Civic League fight against a subdivision in order to protect the beautiful site that is now Drake Park. Today at least several dozen organizations continue this tradition.

How can we minimize our impacts on central Oregon and leave it a little better than we found it?

Be curious and learn about central Oregon history, geography, and the indigenous people who share their home with us. See exhibits and programs at the Warm Springs, High Desert, and Deschutes Historical Museums. Seek out the many great books in local book shops or the public library.

Participate in and support the activities of local land conservation groups. At the Environmental Center in downtown Bend, learn about the Deschutes Land Trust, Friends of Central Cascades Wilderness, Central Oregon Land Watch, and Oregon Natural Desert Association, among others.

Leave No Trace. What if we all left the mountains and desert in a little better shape with each visit? Bring a bag to carry out a few weeds and some litter you find along the way. Study up on Leave No Trace (LNT) practices at LNT.org. Make sure your hiking pole(s) have rubber tips to minimize soil erosion and skewering plants. Maybe try just one pole to halve your impacts.

Choose a Suitable Trail. Over the past 20 years, many central Oregon trails have become much wider, more crowded, and more devoid of flowers and critters. Before leaving home, consider the size of your group and its goals. If you are a large group eager to socialize, try walking wide urban trails or forest roads where you can talk side-by-side without impacting adjacent vegetation or disturbing those seeking quiet solitude in wilder places. Got pups? Take precautions to minimize impacts on wildlife and trail widening. Running? Consider how time, place, and group size affect wildlife and others.

Keep on Rolling. If you arrive at a trailhead with an overflowing parking lot, rather than cramming in and potentially damaging vegetation, simply continue on to another trailhead, usually not far away. You'll likely discover something new, have a nicer experience, and reduce trail and parking lot damage.

Keep Wilderness Secrets. Found a new little-visited trail or secret off-trail gem? Please do not post it online! Try to keep it your secret. Since the rise of the internet, GPS, and SUVs, many once seldom-visited wild places have been overrun. When rarely visited, such places protect wildlife habitat, archeological sites, and human opportunities for adventure, self-discovery, and solitude. Because wilderness is protected for all those values, when a place such as Broken Top tarn is broadcasted online, often with precise GPS route and location descriptions, all those values are degraded, along with ecological ones (see entry for Pumice Moonwort under "Rare"). Authors of guidebooks, web sites, blogs, and magazines that specialize in revealing secret places may find themselves in a special place in wilderness hell where they are condemned to strenuous restoration work, moving big rocks till eternity.

Spread the Word. Share what you learn about LNT and do what you can to help restore the wilds of central Oregon.

~John Schubert

T

Transplanted: *adjective:* reset in another soil or situation

High and Dry in Central Oregon

The sun seeks me out, no shade in sight. I'm at the beginning of my walk and exhausted in this heat. I enjoyed my daily walks at home on the coast; here they are hard work.

The desert landscape is foreign. I have always lived at sea level surrounded by green vegetation. The Oregon Coast where 75 inches of rain falls every year had been my home as a child and we raised our girls there. As a teenager, I lived on the Island of Mallorca in the Mediterranean where my family lived in Puerto Pollensa. I've lived in the Caribbean on the island of St. Croix near the rainforest where frangipani and poinsettias bloomed. The high desert of central Oregon is absent of underbrush, no ferns, and no grass unless irrigated. I hate being landlocked. The air is dry and prickly. My nose bleeds every time I blow it.

We have the Deschutes River here and lakes in the mountains, but if you can see land on the other side, it's not serious water.

The thin dry air blowing against my face causes my eyes to water. My skin itches. I should have brought a hat to shade my eyes and face. The moment I perspire the air dries it. If I can't adapt, how can I help my girls come to grips with the change? They complain of the heat and want to return to the Oregon beaches.

The skitter of the quail in the bushes, the screech of the red tail hawk circling overhead, and the whisper of the wind through the gray-green sage, all are foreign.

I can hear my father's words, "Change is the one constant in our lives. You have to be adaptable to change."

I take along my bird book to identify the birds that live in or pass through this landscape. Their calls are not familiar. Nothing is familiar except the pines, but even they are different. Here the Ponderosa Pines rise high and straight into the ever blue sky. Their eight inch needles differ completely from our pine needles back home. The gnarled Juniper trees grow everywhere. Their spicy sweet odor fills the air and makes me sneeze. The dust invades my body through every pore. Grey squirrels with long bushy tails skitter across the road in front of me, nattering as they hide in the bushes.

I've never lived where irrigation equipment lies in the fields. Every morning our neighbor is out in the field arranging the pipes to water. There is a canal that runs behind our house and fills the pond for irrigating. Wherever the water from the irrigation pipes reaches; the land is green, but if the irrigation water misses an area, it is brown and dry. The sprinklers in our yard keep our lawn green. Their swish, swish, swish as they go back and forth across the grass has a soothing quality. They make it feel as though water is nearby.

I have to look hard to like this new prospect and make it home. Recalling Zane Grey's stories I read as a child. "It was the desert that enchanted Hettie...every time Hettie moved her absorbed gaze from one far point to another...all seemed to change, to magnify in her sight, to draw upon her emotion, and to command her to set her eyes upon the sublime distance...on that stunning mystery of the desert, of that magnificent arid zone which gives this country its name. 'I can only look–and learn to worship,' whispered Hettie." ~Zane Grey, "Nevada"

I can, I know I must, I will find beauty in this new landscape if I see it through different eyes—with Hettie and Zane Grey as my companions.

The view of Mount Bachelor, Broken Top, and the Three Sisters is the prize for walking to the end of the road. They rise into the blue and hold me breathless as I gaze at them. The clouds sail over them as children playing leapfrog. I've seen hundreds of sunsets over the ocean, but this is a different experience. The clouds take on a pink hue that goes from red to orange and finally a dark purple. The mountains hold that glory in their peaks until dusk finally covers us in a cloak of darkness.

~Suzy Beal

T

Twisted: *adjective:* contorted, gnarled, twined, braided, wrenched, tangled, bent

Juniperus occidentalis: a non-accidental tree that is native to central Oregon, spreading roots wide into the heart of the high desert land.

Juniperus occidentalis

The junipers make fists

at the world and its youngsters run amok.
Can you hear the wild arms extending
        into the wind into the night?
Even the beetle in his brownish husk
            begs for saturation.
Juniper skin laps my fingers like cats' tongues
              rasping meat off bones.
Still, the call of conception beats on in the blood
                of our bodies.

Juniper jeers and thrusts out her belly.
Who will bear the bluest berry?
           Winner, gin me up.
(Just so you know, Juniper did not forget to brush
           her hair, she planned it that way.)
I am starting to see how trees are twisted
           through our hearts.
Is this why it hurts to cut them down?
Today I told him, cut all the branches,
           they're blocking our sun.
How ashamed will I be tomorrow?
The junipers flipped me off as I drove,
    shouting hater from their ugly toes.
(I really know how to win them over.)
Later I'll weep among the lost limbs
           that once punched the sky.
Who am I to claim the sun?
Treed heart, you never let go of the sin.
When you are forced to climb the walls, will the leaves
           take their leave of you then?
To reconcile, I do this thing: I stand with the junipers,
           twisting my face
and when people drive by, we wave middle fingers
while squinting up at the sun.

~Danielle Gosselin

"Place dictates who we are and how we see."

—Linn Ulmann, qtd. in "Before You Can Write a Good Plot, You Need to Write a Good Place" by Joe Fassler. *The Atlantic.* 23 Apr. 2014. Accessed 15 Sept. 2020.

U

Ulali: *noun:* Chinook Wawa word for berry or huckleberry

Tumalo Falls

The third time I went out to Tumalo Falls, I walked almost all the way down to the pool where the water crashes into Tumalo Creek. The steep path was narrow, and it made me nervous. It was overgrown with sage, slick with spray, sometimes gravely or muddy, and there were large volcanic boulders that I imagined a body (head attached, of course) would hit on its long tumble down to the creek below. Mostly I was nervous because my seven-year-old and ten-year-old grandsons were also on the path and they seemed oblivious to any danger.

We were all headed to the base of the falls because my daughter was going to get married beneath them. Only she and her partner, their dog, and the minister walked all the way to where the water thundered. The noise was tremendous. I'm sure they chose the falls so they could say their vows in private.

Hikers who were heading out stopped other hikers who were heading in, asking them to wait the ten minutes or so for the ceremony to take place, which they kindly did. The falls are just fourteen miles west of Bend, Oregon, after all, where bumper stickers say, "Be Nice. You're in Bend." The rest of the wedding party—five adults, including me, and two children—perched precariously above the falls, the mist rising, the sunshine falling, and took pictures with cell phones. Except for me. I didn't take pictures. I watched the children. Ten minutes is a long time for boys to stand still and not throw rocks into a ravine.

How high are the falls? 97 feet some say although the North West Waterfall Survey of 2010 measured them at 89. They are fed by glacial melt and in turn feed the Deschutes River, after which the beer is named. They are surrounded by sage and juniper and if , instead of detouring as we did, you stay on the main path from the parking lot, which is wider and maintained and has a much gentler incline, you will find a viewing platform, a bathroom, and a map of the 7.4 mile loop trail that circles past alpine lakes and several other waterfalls through the watershed for the city of Bend, which is not really a city.

According to one source, it is thought—by whom? passive voice reveals a lot—that the name "Tumalo" comes from the Klamath Indian word "temolo" meaning "wild plum." Or it might mean "ground fog," from "temola," or "icy water," from "tumallowa." The geographical historian, Lewis A. MacArthur, wrote, "Any of the above explanations might fit the facts, so there you are."

For a short while, in the late 1800s, the falls were called Laidlaw Falls, after W.A. Laidlaw who, along with the Carey Act, encouraged white settlers to "reclaim" these arid lands and promised them irrigation so they could do so. Like the falls, the town of Tumalo was, for a time, named Laidlaw, but when the irrigation project failed, the falls and the town were renamed, and Laidlaw was hung in effigy.

The falls are within the traditional territory of the Molalla tribes, who traded with the Chinookans to the north, the Klamaths to the south, the Paiutes to the east, and the Kalapuyans in the west. A linguistic map suggests the Molallas occupied the Cascades and parts of the Deschutes Basin. Their name is a corruption of the Chinook Wawa word "ulali" meaning berry or huckleberry. Why is it that a Chinook word names them, that a people don't name themselves but are named by others?

Their winter houses were made of cedar planks and hemlock, dug partly into the earth for insulation. They had round sweat lodges made of the same materials. In summer, they ranged the entire Cascades, gathering berries and wild plums, hazel nuts and camas root, wild onion and tubers, fishing the rivers for steelhead and salmon, hunting elk and deer and rabbit. The men often wore deer heads to stalk their prey and the women wore loose trousers made of deer hide. Little is known of the southern Molalla.

Although their origin stories locate their creation at the base of Mount Hood, they had small winter villages near Oregon City and Salem, and at the base of Mt. Jefferson. In warmer weather, they left their homes to hunt and gather and trade throughout the Willamette Valley as well as throughout the Cascades. They must have had sacred places. When Coyote created them, he foretold that they would be "good men and good hunters," that they would "think all the time they are on a hunt."

By 1856, the Molalla had signed two treaties, after which most were removed to the Grand Ronde Indian Reservation with many of the other tribes. The state of Oregon has a long history of forced removal of tribes to reservations; one such removal was known as the Umpqua Trail of Tears. None of the treaties were honored.

Now, according to the website for Oregon State Parks and Recreation, Tumalo Falls' "location makes it an ideal stepping stone for any type of outdoor activity you could possibly dream of: lush green golf courses, clear blue-ribbon trout streams, pristine alpine lakes, miles upon miles of challenging yet scenic hiking and mountain bike trails. . ."

And, of course, weddings. The bride wore a short white sheath and flip flops, the groom, Bermuda shorts and a white button-down shirt. Their smiles were luminous.

~Beth Alvarado

U

Undercurrent: *noun:* a hidden feeling or viewpoint contrary to the prevailing mood

Prineville: Word on the Street
A Call and Response

As a mental health therapist working in the heart of Crook County, only blocks from the protests and counter protests of Black Lives Matter, Back the Blue, Save Our Children and many other fringe elements concerned with the state of the union, I wrote this piece not as my subjective, personal experience as a white, cisgender, middle class woman in our rural town, but as a vessel that collects and holds the stories of our community members for safekeeping.

These are some of the words they've shared, whether in the quiet, neutral, calm of a therapeutic space or as they shout them across the great divide of "main street America." I wanted to represent the polarization occurring here over the past few months during the demonstrations which typically straddle Highway 126 as it moves from east to west through town.

I also wanted to recognize the dialectic quality of the discourse in Prineville these days with the AND oriented in the center of the page. This placement on the page also represents the thoroughfare which has become a demilitarized zone in our town.

This DMZ is where the vast majority of people move—through the yelling and aggression—trying to exist in the liminal space of day-to-day living. "Next civil war" has been uttered in the local and national conversation, but what many know to be true is that they do not want that here, if at all. There is a strong undercurrent of those looking to live happily and peacefully in this ruggedly, beautiful area honoring and acknowledging the history of past generations while looking to the sunrise each morning as a symbol of hope and growth on the horizon.

Prineville	AND	Prinetucky
Main Street	AND	Highway 126
Back the Blue	AND	Black Lives Matter
I Am Angry	AND	I Am Angry
Terrorists	AND	Peaceful Protests
Militias	AND	Terrorists
"Go Back Home"	AND	"I live Here"
#MAGA	AND	#ACAB
We Don't Need This	AND	You Need This
I am Scared	AND	I am Scared
IT isn't a Problem	AND	YOU are the Problem
All Lives Matter	AND	No Justice, No Peace
I Don't Understand	AND	I Don't Understand
Raising Flags	AND	Destroying Flags
Nooses Hanging	AND	Fingers Flying
I feel Threatened	AND	I feel Threatened
Save OUR Children	AND	And THESE children?
This isn't Bend	AND	This isn't Bend
God Wouldn't Approve	AND	God Wouldn't Approve
Thou Shalt Love Thy Neighbor	AND	Love is Love
Communist	AND	Fascists
I want Better	AND	I want Better
Karens	AND	Snowflakes
Americans	AND	Americans
Manassas	AND	Bull Run
We the People	AND	Power to the People
Trust No One	AND	Trust No One
I Want Safety	AND	I Want Safety
CC Strong	AND	Redneck Pride

Hardworking, Salt of the Earth	AND	Uneducated
See Me, Hear Me	AND	See Me, Hear Me
White Savior Complex	AND	White Guilt
.8 % of the Community	AND	Still Relevant
J.E.D.I.	AND	Take a Knee
"This isn't Portland"	AND	"This is a Hick Town"
It's an Election Year	AND	It's an Election Year
Misrepresentation	AND	More Representation
Three Percenters	AND	The Ninety Nine Percent
George Soros	AND	George Floyd
Kyle Rittenhouse	AND	Michael Forest Reinhoel
First Responders are Family	AND	Defund the Police
We Want Peace	AND	We Want Change
They Don't Get Rural Ore	AND	Kate Brown
Families First	AND	My Family Doesn't Feel Safe
We Have to Teach Them Right	AND	I am Afraid to go to School
They are hardworking folks	AND	They could deport my family
Build Walls	AND	Tear it Down
US	AND	Them
Them	AND	Us
Generational Trauma, Poverty, Substance abuse	AND	Generational Trauma, Poverty, Substance Use
I Hurt	AND	I Hurt
There is History Here	AND	There is a Future Here
Don't Tread on Me	AND	We are All in this Together
Freedom	AND	Safety
Proud Boys	AND	Antifa
Ego	AND	Ego

You Don't Speak for Me	AND	You Don't Speak for Me
Yelling	AND	Yelling
Proud to be From Here	AND	Ashamed to be From There
My Home	AND	My Home
Vote For My White Man	AND	Vote For My White Man
2020	AND	2020

~Robyn Loxley

V

Vector: *verb*: to change the direction of

In the darkness the light starts to shine

On July 7, 2014, I woke at 7 am, sick and shaky. I had just got off a six-day bender of utter demoralization. I was $400 short on my rent and didn't know what I was going to do. I knew if I could get ready for work before 8 and to the bar, I could remedy my sour stomach and shakiness enough to go to work.

At the bar, it was dark and dim as if time had stopped the night before. The poker machines to my right were lit up and flashing, welcoming me. I saw the bartender Katie already had my drink started—16 ounces of champagne, a splash of orange juice, and a shot of blueberry vodka. After I sucked my first drink down, I started to feel better.

I went to work and then to a doctor's appointment at Deschutes County Public Health that I'd scheduled because of what had happened on my six-day bender. I walked through the automatic doors at the clinic and met a doctor with soft blue eyes and highlighted blonde hair. Her lab coat was like any other doctor's, but underneath she wore a hippie skirt with an earthy print. On her feet she wore Dansko clogs.

"What's the reason for your visit today?" she asked.

I told her everything about my incomprehensible behaviors during my bender. For once in my entire life, I told the truth about my drinking.

After I was done, she looked at me and asked me one simple question: "Can you stop drinking?"

"Yes," I lied. "I can. It's not a problem for me."

"Good," she said, and then she looked at me simply and sweetly.

"My boyfriend," I said, "he has that problem. He goes to Alcoholics Anonymous."

"My husband's an alcoholic," she said, nodding, "he's in recovery."

"Well, that's good. I hope my boyfriend can stay sober, too. It's a real problem for him."

We talked a bit more, and then the appointment was over.

When I got home, I called my best friend Nancy. We had pitchers of margaritas to help cure my hangover, and I told her my woes. The question the doctor had asked me, *can you stop drinking?* rang in my mind over and over. The answer was no, I thought to myself. The jig is up. I can't stop drinking.

After Nancy and I said goodnight, I thought to myself, do I listen to the monster of the disease, calling me towards eventual darkness and shameful behavior, or do I listen to, and honestly answer, the small, sweet voice of that doctor?

***

I have a genetic disposition that causes me to be an alcoholic. Once I start drinking, I can't stop. I started drinking at age thirteen in part because of years of abuse from men. I was raped at 15 by my boyfriend whom I thought I could trust when I ran away from home. I was married at age 25 to a man who was physically, mentally, emotionally, and verbally abusive. After he held me down and choked me, I got up the courage to leave him. I then put myself through cosmetology college and worked two jobs.

After that, you would think my life would have gotten better, but in fact, that's when my drinking really started to escalate. When I was 27, I dated another abusive man for about three years. He was the most violent offender of them all. For so long, it was much easier to drown out my pain with alcohol than to reach out for help and look at the traumatic things that had happened to me in the past.

***

The next day, I went with my boyfriend to my first AA meeting at Eastmont church in Bend. The people were so welcoming and kind. They didn't judge me, they just offered me encouragement, support, and love. At that first meeting, someone asked if anyone was in their first 24 hours of sobriety, and I said, "my name is Dannie," and, for the first time in my life, I said, "I am an alcoholic."

***

I have been sober for more than six years because of that one question that sweet doctor asked me: can you stop drinking? It's only by the grace of God, but I stand here today. I am a member of society, I am self employed, and I am an educator. I am a loving daughter and mother, and I am a friend, but most of all, I am a beautiful child of God and a grateful member of AA. Thanks to my higher power and AA, I have my life back and it is manageable. Not every day is easy, but my worst day sober is far better than my best day drunk. My hope in writing this is to inspire anyone who is struggling with addiction, domestic violence, or abuse of any kind. A dear friend once shared this quote with me: *What if I fall? Oh, but my darling, what if you fly?*

~Dannie Garrett

"This is wheel country."

—Anonymous

Whistle pig: *noun:* large stout-bodied ground squirrel

Yellow-bellied Marmot: *Marmota Flaviventris*

Marmot (mar'met) noun 1. Any bushy-tailed, stocky, rodent of the genus Marmota (derivative of marmotter, meaning to mutter, murmur). Colloquially called rock chuck or whistle pig. Spend approximately 80% of their lives underground, often hibernating from August to March. Found on slopes with a mix of rock and grass throughout central Oregon including the v-shaped area surrounding the bushy Bend sign between Highway 20 and Division Street, the Old Mill District, the sports fields at Bend and Mountain View High Schools, and in the rocky cliffs across the Deschutes River from Farewell Bend Park.

Yellow-bellied Marmot

On snowy days, driving by Mountain View's playing fields, I think of the hibernating rock chucks. They are deep in their winter burrows hidden among the snow-covered rocks. I wonder if they have soft bedding in their burrows. Do they shape nests from neighborhood flora: tall grasses of fescue, fuzzy blooms of Russian sage, petals of lupine? Do they forage thyme for scent? Or do they sleep on hardened dirt with their thick fur providing softness? Are they curled around themselves or sprawled out, belly up, legs splayed?

I envy their hibernation; the stillness, its depth. What must it be like to wake, to rise after months underneath? In March, I saw one at the entry of its burrow, snow still covering the ground. It looked dazed, its fur matted and greasy. But it sniffed the air as if inhaling everything: the barely emerged shoots of grass, the mud, the snow. How is hunger when you rise? Is there memory?

Imagining the rock chucks deep in rest has saved me. I need the sweetness. I need to know as we burn our world, somewhere nearby sage grouse dance only for each other, somewhere fawns are hidden in wildflowers, somewhere a rock chuck is rising, not directed by thought but by the primitive urges, the primitive knowing of its body.

It is not just sweetness I need. I know, in the fall, elk will rut to the point of injury, even death. I know the crow in my yard is scavenging the nests of the scrub jays and squirrels for soft pink bodies. I hear the protests of the parents, see the jay's aerial dives. I know the raccoons will eat the tadpoles in my small pond before even their legs emerge. This gives me comfort. Our greed, short-sightedness, destruction, lust. We are not so different. We act on primitive urges. To our detriment, to the world's detriment. We hold lofty our frontal lobe, our ability to have forethought, to understand consequences. Yet our actions often come from the body, the nerves. Feelings of longing and belonging more driving, more urgent than common sense.

When I watch hummingbirds— oh nests of spider silk— fiercely claim a flower patch, chasing and knocking each other to the ground, driving competitors out of the yard despite countless blooms, I recognize we are a part of things. Our struggles are not just human, but the struggles of being alive. What is mine? Is there enough? How will I eat and feed my babies? Where will I shelter? I feel a softness there, a kinship. Love. And then I want to protect it all. Make room for everything. Love a more workable, actionable place than guilt, disgust, shame.

In summer, when I see the rock chucks scanning the deep green playing fields, waiting for the teams to leave so they can eat and get fat on the abundant grasses, I know: there is enough. There is enough. There can be enough.

~Kathy Lawrence

Wildflower: *noun*: the specialized part bearing the reproductive structures of an uncultivated plant or the plant bearing it

Bigelow's Monkeyflower: *Diplacus bigelovii* (formerly known as *Mimulus bigelovii*)

Annual wildflower native to dry areas of the West, Bigelow's Monkeyflower thrives in a shrub-steppe habitat and is often seen growing in sandy areas from April through June. This magenta wildflower grows from 1" to 10" tall. The leaves grow opposite each other, and are oblong, ending in sharp points. The bright flowers are reminiscent of Snapdragon flowers, with magenta-pink petals and yellow, open throats. Often seen blooming after spring rainfall.

Look closely, pay attention. When the April skies are dull and you can't see the friendly sun or the stately mountains, when you are tired of the spiritless green-ish-brown of winter, and weary of the dust that the wind rudely blows into your face, a spatter of rain will come.

Following the rain, Lilliputian seedlings will grow, bud, bloom. Then, look down. Step carefully. Between the gnarled grey juniper trees and the smudged sagebrush, you will begin to see flowers. Wee ones. Bright pink-purple ones. You'll be surprised, because the snow-cracked volcanic dirt seems so inhospitable, and the space surrounding the flowers so bare, and full of nothing. Peer more closely, and you'll see that each flower has a yellow throat, singing straight up to the sometimes-sun, sometimes-snow, sometimes-rain, sometimes-flat sky. Before finding out this flower's name - Bigelow's Monkeyflower - I had always just hung it on a coat hook in my brain as "that tiny bold tough petite bright pink flower that implausibly blooms in the unlikeliest of places, and I try hard not to step on." A brave plant, this Bigelow's Monkeyflower, with the flowering part often fully half of the entirety of the plant itself, it defies logic, growing on, fulfilling its part to bring beauty to the early spring desert. No matter how many springs pass, I always crouch down and gaze at this minute wildflower, wondering how such sweetness could spring from the stony ground. Snap your fingers, and the Monkeyflowers are gone. The warm days of summer approach, and all that remains of the diminutive beauty of the Monkeyflowers is a memory, and seeds, scattered in the driest dust.

-Grace King

Exchange: *noun*: reciprocal giving and receiving

Multicultural Kitchen

We meet in the kitchen of my cozy house on the west side of Bend.

For those that know Bend, Oregon, the "west side" awakens images of beautiful, affluent, brand-spankin' new homes. My kitchen, however, has been waiting 25 years to be remodeled, and it will have to wait a while longer. The paint is peeling from the cabinets whose doors continually sag from their hinges before being screwed in tight once again. After all, these cabinets have to serve as poster boards for vocabulary words from the eight languages being studied in my household. They'll have to hang on a little longer!

For many that know Bend, another image that may come to mind is a whitewashed lack of diversity. My kitchen, on the other hand, has been graced by people from China, Japan, Chile, Mexico, Germany, Columbia, Russia, the Ukraine, as well as both North and South Korea. These are not visitors. They live in central Oregon. They cook your food, clean your clothes, tow your cars, take care of your children, wash your dishes, and make sure you are safe during medical procedures.

These are the people who come into my kitchen and share a meal with me. They also share their language, culture, and their stories. And in doing so, they inevitably steal a piece of my heart. A piece that I will never get back, and yet somehow I know that there is more room in my heart every time I give a piece of it away.

The walls in my kitchen have heard their stories: stories of being imprisoned for religious beliefs, being tortured for being on the wrong side of a border, having bullets whiz through the living room window, starvation, forced labor, and so much more. What you see on the news, I hear about from my friends. Some have come straight from a war zone, others from a country whose policy is to imprison and torture parents because their children have emigrated. Then there are those that continue to hide Christians even though their family members have been imprisoned for such activity. Representatives of international political conflicts sit quietly and peacefully in my kitchen. These stories are not merely flashing on my cell phone screen, they are flesh and blood.

Have I wept with these international heart-thieves? Yes!

Have I spent sleepless nights, wondering how to help their families, wishing that I could do oh-so-much more than is in my power? Of course! But my kitchen walls hear much more than weeping and heartbreak. In fact, my multi-cultural kitchen is overwhelmingly full of laughter and love, much more than the sorrow that must be. Why is this? It is because I have the unbelievably profound opportunity of praying with these remarkable people. By sharing their fears, their heartbreak, and their struggles I can then share their joys, their victories, and the grace that washes over and through their lives. All of this in a little, worn down kitchen in Bend, Oregon. Here I learn again and again that Oregon is a special place: a place where we can live, work, grow, practice our religion, and have a meal each and every day. A place where my diverse friends can walk down the street without fear, where they can play with their children and drink a cup of coffee with a friend.

Bend is beautiful, and this beauty is compounded exponentially in the faces of the friends in my kitchen. Never have I met such grateful, joyful, optimistic people! Although we may weep together, the tears never have the last word. Instead they lead us to a deep, lasting joy that shines through the blue skies of the high desert and lights up the hearts of those in my multi-cultural kitchen.

~Janet Gesme

"The [pioneer] grave was marked with rocks piled a foot or so in height. Laying at the grave was a pint jar with a piece of paper in it. Written on the paper was the name of a eleven year old girl, believed to have the last name of Steins. The site was destroyed when the Fox Trailer Court was built."

—Carol & Edna Boyd qtd. in *Small Cemeteries & Lone Graves of Deschutes Co., Oregon.* Bend Geneological Society, Inc., 1999. p. 35.

Y

Yen: *noun*: a strong desire or propensity

Home: generally defined as the place of residence, where one lives permanently, a location of comfort, security or love.

Home

There is a familiarity in the texture,
especially in shadows,
whispering, "where have you been?"

It smells like vanilla in the ponderosa,
dirt in a rainstorm,
sage underfoot in the caliche-riddled basin.

Sounds like ears ringing in the bare cirque,
an echo of a far-off rock-fall,
sand raining onto the old shed.

Tastes like salt hitting the edge of my cracked mouth.
A hint of iron mixed with the muted sweetness
of last year's pine needles.

A young wolf breaks through the flaxen grass;
she steals a sideways glance,
and we silently pass the code.

A wave of unseen fireflies
strum my nervous system,
and a warm embrace follows, cell to cell.

~Catherine Gockley

Z

Zumba: *noun*: an exercise fitness program created by Columbian dancer and choreographer Alberto "Beto" Pérez

Zumba

In the winter of 2014, a few days after I arrived in La Pine from Chile to live near my mom, I got invited to a community event at the elementary school. I met this beautiful, kind lady named Rebecca, who was my son's English teacher. She invited me to a Latino women's reunion in Bend, which I gladly accepted. During the reunion I heard a lot of women say they struggled with dieting, and that they didn't work out because they thought the gym was boring and they didn't feel included there. On top of that, these women had little kids and no way of leaving them with a babysitter or the dad. Mexican husbands are very possessive and they don't allow the wife to go anywhere without the little ones. As a child in Mexico, I had dancing lessons from a young age and I had performed on stage many, many times. For a long time I wanted to be a professional dancer. After I heard the women speak, I offered them Zumba classes for free twice a week.

I started with ten women. At the first class they were shy and uncertain, but after a few classes they began to let themselves go, to get more confident, to improve their bodies, and to be happy. After a few months, I had over 50 women in class. They never imagined themselves performing on a stage in front of hundreds of people, but they have danced at El Festival de Las Culturas in Redmond three times since I started teaching.

After six years of teaching Zumba classes in Bend, I still have lots of people. Many of my students have followed me all these years. They feel comfortable, welcome, and part of my class. During Zumba my girls enjoy our Latin music wrapping around their bodies. The sensuality of their hips moving to the rhythm of bachata makes them feel sexy and confident. The energy of merengue and quebradita makes them feel powerful. Cumbia and samba make them feel cheerful and happy. My girls have experienced a tremendous change in their health, their bodies, and their souls. My dream of becoming a professional dancer was impossible at my age, but I realized that being a Zumba instructor was good enough for me because it allowed me to improve these women's health and lives. I feel honored to be part of their lives.

-Karla Aguilera

bla**Z**e

Blaze: *noun*: a trail marker; a mark made on a tree by chipping off a piece of the bark

Breaking Trail *North Shevlin Park*

The dog swoops
in and out of snow
like a heavy black fish, my skis fall in,
two feet, no three, no wonder
we're the only ones here.
Push, step, step,
I shift my weight forward
in snow up to my thighs. This
isn't skiing but a slow waltz, a working prayer,
my thanks for the sun, the 18 degrees,
the outlandish, strange figures of snow on
the cliffs, the pines, the creek slugging along by my side.
The dog burrows in, surfaces, sneezes, settles
to step along on the backs of my skis. I'm sweating

through my long underwear, up the short hill,
push, step, step, down, under the trees dropping their
wet bundles of snow, it's getting warm,
step after step, past the meadow
where late November we saw
the cougar kill, the fuss of blood on frozen grass.
The big mule deer is just a spine
and some ribs now, under the snow, as
we step past the crowd of junipers, scrambling,
half rolling up the next hill, and finally
the pond.   Wait. Is that all there is?
This pond in the shadows, iced over, the white clearing,
the old road ahead subsumed
in snow.   I look back at our track, the narrow,
wandering trail is what we have
to show for ourselves,
our witness, yes. This is all. It's enough.

-Cat Finney

Some of the people who inhabited Millican -

Huff family homesteaded about 1913
P. B. Johnson & family
J. A. & Mitchel & Pearl Smith
Billy Rahn
Lloyd Owerns
Floyd and Annie Van Cleave homestead in 1914
Hooper & Irene Dyer from Iowa came in the 1920s
Edgbert & Leona (Dolly) Dryer about 1915
Ernest, Elmer & Howard Dyer
Floyd Stookey
Bill Frost
Kigers
Levis Smith
Glesses
Evans
Vernon Clevenger
Mellin

—from *Small Cemeteries & Lone Graves of Deschutes Co., Oregon.*
Bend Geneological Society, Inc., 1999. p. 33.

Epilogue

And so, after being pulled and prodded, fawned and fussed over by a team of well-meaning obsessives— *I don't recommend it* — I go on, my jacket snugged tight, to try my luck in high desert bookstores and libraries, waiting rooms and classrooms, coffee shops, desktops, parking lots, and laptops. I aim to ask questions and listen to everyone I meet.

As for my editors, they hope that, after reading me, you'll think about what central Oregon means to you, and then write it down, and then maybe even submit it for Volume Two or Three or Four of *Placed*, because, you know, this collection is only a beginning. When it comes to stories of this place, and the generations of people to tell them, we're brushing up against something like, I don't know, maybe infinity.

So let's get started on the next volume: *What does this place mean to you? What is your central Oregon story? Will you tell it?*

Will you?

Contributor Biographies

La Pine, Oregon resident **Karla Aguilera** earned a bachelor's degree in American Studies from OSU-Cascades in 2020, where she earned a Culture of Writing award. In 2019 she was selected to present original work at the OSU Humanities Conference. She has taught Zumba at various locations in central Oregon, and aspires to study law.

Beth Alvarado is the author of *Anxious Attachments,* winner of the 2020 Oregon Book Award for Creative Nonfiction, and *Jillian in the Borderlands: A Cycle of Rather Dark Tales,* and two earlier books. She migrated from Tucson, Arizona to the high desert of Bend, Oregon in 2016. www.bethalvarado.com.

Suzy Beal spent 25 years helping seniors put their stories to paper and this year just finished her own memoir. She writes personal essays and is currently studying poetry. Her work has appeared on truestorieswelltold.com, Story Circle Network, 101words and Central Oregon Writers Guild.

Alex Borgen is an interdisciplinary artist interested in fieldwork, importance of transitional or liminal spaces—conceptual, physical, and temporal— and the ways in which we become the terrain that sustains us. Each of her art projects results in a coinciding manuscript. Borgen has shown nationally and internationally and holds an MFA in Interdisciplinary Book & Paper Arts from Columbia College Chicago. www.alexborgen.com

Krayna Castelbaum, dedicated Poetry Instigator, has been a passionate facilitator of creative self-expression for over 30 years. She writes poetry, offers monthly Poetry Playshops, publishes Poem of the Month, and collaborates with other creatives to enrich the central Oregon community she calls home. krayna@clearlenscoaching.com

Irene Cooper is the author of *Committal,* a speculative spy-fy novel from Vegetarian Alcoholic Press, & *spare change,* poetry from Finishing Line Press. Poems, stories & reviews appear online and in print. Irene teaches creative writing, co-edits *The Stay Project* & lives with her people & a corgi in Oregon. www.irenecooperwrites.com

Mike Cooper holds an MFA from Oregon State University. He is president of the Central Oregon Writers Guild and teaches writing at Central Oregon Community College and Oregon State University-Cascades, as well as creative writing workshops at The Workhouse, a local artists' collective, the Deschutes Public Library,

and COCC Community Learning. www.blankpag-
esworkshops.com

Ginny Contento is a writer, healthcare interpreter, and
Spanish teacher in Bend, Oregon.

Sarah Sennott Cyr's work has appeared in *Newsweek*,
*The Boston Globe, Boston Magazine, Cosmopolitan, ART-
News* and *Brevity*. She began a daily writing practice in
2014 after reading Natalie Goldberg's *Writing Down the
Bones*. Since then, she's studied extensively with Goldberg including a year-long writing intensive at the Upa-
ya Zen Center in Santa Fe taught in collaboration with
author Robert Wilder. www.sarahcyr.com

Angelo DiNocenzo is a father, an observationalist, and
an eternal student of the arts and sciences. He enjoys
the cyclic turn of the seasons, with the potential of nature's perfection. Angelo is a collector of perspectives—
Blooms of thought, that Fertilize the mind, will rest as
Seeds of knowledge.

AJ Doherty has been crafting words on napkins and laptops since the 1990s, sipping pints and writing plays in
pubs in England, studying Irish literature and creative
writing at an Iowa Writers Workshop at Trinity College,
where she fell in love with her husband and Dublin. Find
more of AJ's writing on Medium.com.

Nicholas Famoso received his bachelor's (BS) in geology from South Dakota School of Mines and Technology,

and his master's (MS) in geological sciences and doctorate (PhD) in earth sciences from University of Oregon. Nick is currently Chief of Paleontology and Museum Curator at John Day Fossil Beds National Monument.

Cat Finney is a poet and an Associate Librarian of Collections/Acquisitions at Central Oregon Community College in Bend, Oregon.

Dannie Garrett is a stylist, educator, and blogger in the beauty industry. A member of a personal narrative writing workshop at Saving Grace in Bend, Oregon, she read her work at the World Muse Conference in Bend in 2016.

Janet Gesme is a musician, translator, teacher, wife, and mother. She has played in orchestras across the country and enjoys speaking German, Russian, Spanish, French, and Korean. She feels blessed by the opportunity to translate Christoper Schacht's *Around the World on 50 Bucks* and Martin Schleske's *The Sound of Life's Unspeakable Beauty.*

Catherine Gockley is a backcountry ranger, field scientist, and writer. She lives at tree-line.

Central Oregon is one of **Danielle Gosselin's** favorite places in the world. She is honored to be included in this encyclopedia. Danielle is currently a traveller bound for the Bolivian Amazon where she will work with wildlife. From the jungle to the junipers, it has always come down to the trees.

Kake Huck is a desultory poet and artist living with her spouse and two poodles. Her work has won a couple of prizes but not recently. More of her poems may be found in a couple of anthologies as well as the books Murderous Glamour and Sentenced to Venice. https:// dancingmoonpress.com/project/sentenced-to-venice/

Grace King is a third generation Oregonian who has lived in Bend since childhood. For her, the flora and fauna of central Oregon are like old friends. She loves language and writes to capture memories and moments of her experiences traveling and observing the natural world.

Kathy Lawrence is a therapist living in Portland, Oregon. She spent one dog year in central Oregon and loves the marmots, wildflower meadows, and green waters. She has led writing groups with the Deschutes Public Library and Write Around Portland.

Brigitte Lewis is a writer born in Gold Country, destined for speculation. Her work has appeared or is forthcoming from *DIAGRAM, Hobart, The Southampton Review, The Bellingham Review,* and more. Her chapbook, *Origin Stories,* comes out December 2020 from *Iron Horse Review.* https://www.brigitteelewis.com/writing

Kennedy Lovette is a 20-year-old college student getting her degree in American Studies. She grew up in Sisters, Oregon. She enjoys listening to true crime podcasts when she is not preoccupied with school. Kennedy is a biracial woman who has learned to navigate life in an area that is lacking diversity.

Robyn Loxley is a veteran of the United States Army Reserve, mother to a large blended family, Oregon State University graduate and mental health therapist located in Prineville, Oregon. In her free time, Robyn enjoys reading, rock hounding, taking photos and spending time outdoors with family and animals.

Anastasia Lugo-Mendez is a central Oregon writer focused on short and longform fiction. Past stories have been featured in Utah State University publications *Sink Hollow* (2017) and *Scribendi* (2016).

Renee Patrick worked with the Oregon Natural Desert Association to develop the Oregon Desert Trail. When she's not sleeping on the ground and covering 30 miles a day, she can be found packrafting, skiing, biking, or hiking around central Oregon.

Ben Paulus' most recent work appears in the anthology *Science-Based Vulnerability: Scientists and Poets #RESIST*. You can watch him read at the Loft Literary Center in Minneapolis at https://www.youtube.com/watch?v=4vu8-I6dyUU. Find out more at www.ben-paulus.com.

Charmane Powers graduated from The Evergreen State College in Olympia, Washington, focusing on birds and botany. She moved to Bend, Oregon in 1989 and has been a botanist with the U.S. Forest Service on the Deschutes National Forest since 1990. She has been charmed by the pumice moonwort ever since.

Marina Richie is a nature writer and blogger at www.marinarichie.com. Her work appears in *Post Road, Think Journal, Columbia Insight, Appalachian Trail Journeys, Birdwatching,* and *Vision magazines, National Wildlife, Audubon, Center for Humans and Nature, Musepaper,* and *Tiny Seed Literary Journal.* She is the author of two children's books: *Bird Feats* and *Bug Feats.*

The only thing **Ellen Santasiero** likes better than making essays, memoirs, collages, plays, fictions, and safe spaces for learning is making them with others. Her work has appeared in *The Stay Project, The Sun,* and *High Desert Journal,* among others, and is forthcoming in *7x7.* She teaches literature and writing at OSU-Cascades in Bend, Oregon. ellensantasiero.com

John Schubert's career as a Trails Specialist and Wilderness Ranger spanned 45 years from the North Cascades to Lake Baikal, via nine states. Settled in his native Oregon since 1987, John worked 27 years for the Deschutes National Forest. He co-founded Commute Options and served on the Bend City Council in Oregon. See his trails presentation at DeschutesLandTrust.org and blog posts at PCTA.org

Leila Shepherd, a native of North Carolina, has been making central Oregon her home for 17 years. The beauty of the high desert landscape makes her heart sing. She thrives on supporting elders, dabbling in art and writing projects, and tending her succulent garden and native plants for pollinators.

Siobhan Sullivan enjoys combining her knowledge of science with her love of culture in her writing. She is creating three children's novels set in Oregon's high desert. Siobhan often shares her encounters with nature, history, and culture on her blog, Bend Branches, and in the High Desert Museum's volunteer newsletter. https://bendbranches.com/

Alex Tretbar is a librarian and GED tutor at Deer Ridge Correctional Institution. He graduated from the University of Kansas with degrees in journalism and English, and is currently at work on a book-length poem about tic-tac-toe.

Local food and farming is in **Laurie Wayne's** blood – she found out only recently that her grandfather maintained a two-acre Victory Garden in World War II. Laurie has operated an organic farm and started community gardens, food hubs, and farmers markets in the Pacific Northwest over the last 25 years.

A retired social worker, **Janet Whitney** has been an activist for social justice in Bend, Oregon for 25 years. In addition to advocacy work with a variety of nonprofits, she enjoys writing poetry and haiku.

In 1976, **Bob Woodward** transitioned from retailer to a writer/photographer specializing in outdoor sports, travel and adventure with editor stints at Times-Mirror Magazines, The New York Times Magazine Group and CBS. A 42-year resident of Bend, Oregon, Woodward served on the Bend City Council (Mayor 1997 to 1999) and on the Bend Metro Parks board of directors.

Randy Workman is a free-lance writer. His articles, essays and poetry have appeared in *The Seattle Times, Los Angeles Daily News Sunday Magazine*, and in *433*, a daily magazine of art, literature and politics.

Appendix

Page 13: Percentages of people of color in central Oregon: Crook County: 5.3%, Deschutes County: 5.9%, Jefferson County: 24.1 (2019 US Census).

Page 21: Central Oregon's dry forests are fire adapted, shaped by low-intensity fires occurring every two to 25 years. In the last decade (2010 - 2020), Oregon wildfires have burned between 30,000 to over 200,000 acres per year (Oregon Forest Resources Institute). The Oregon Department of Forestry has identified over 750,000 acres of Wildland Urban Interface, areas in which homes border undeveloped wildland vegetation and are at increased risk of wildfire (Conservation Biology Institute), across Bend, Sisters, Redmond, and Prineville.

Page 43: The largest cat in North America. A solitary ambush predator, nocturnal or crepuscular, it is adaptable and found in most American habitat types (Wikipedia 6-22-2019). Oregon has a population of approximately 6,000 mountain lions, with the highest densities occurring in the Blue Mountains and in the southwestern Cascades.

Page 59: For more on the belted kingfisher, visit Cornell Lab of Ornithology's All About Birds website.

Page 73: References
Albright III, L. B., M. O. Woodburne, T. J. Fremd, C. C. Swisher III, B. J. MacFadden, and G. R. Scott. 2008. "Revised chronostratigraphy and biostratigraphy of the John Day Formation (Turtle Cove and Kimberly Members), Oregon, with implications for updated calibration of the Arikareean North American Land Mammal Age." The Journal of Geology 116: 211-237.

Bestland, E. A., M. S. Forbes, E. S. Krull, G. J. Retallack, and T. J. Fremd. 2008. "Stratigraphy, paleopedology, and geochemistry of the middle Miocene Mascall Formation (Type area, central Oregon, USA)." PaleoBios 28: 41-61.

Bestland, E. A., P. E. Hammond, D. L. S. Blackwell, M. A. Kays, G. J. Retallack, and J. Stimac. 1999. "Geologic framework of the Clarno Unit, John Day Fossil Beds National Monument: Central Oregon." Oregon Geology 61: 3-19.

Chaney, R. W. 1959. "Miocene floras of the Columbia Plateau. Part I, Composition and interpretation." Carnegie Institution of Washington Publication 617: 1-134.

Dillhoff, R. M., T. A. Dillhoff, R. E. Dunn, J. A. Myers, and C. A. E. Strömberg. 2009. Cenozoic paleobotany of the John Day Basin, central Oregon. Vol. 15, in Volcanoes to Vineyards: Geologic Field Trips through the Dynamic Landscape of the Pacific Northwest, edited by J. E. O'Connor, R. J. Dorsey and I. P. Madin, 135-164. Geological Society of America Field Guide.

Downs, T. 1956. "The Mascall fauna from the Miocene of Oregon." University of California Publications in Geological Sciences 31: 199-354.

Enlows, H. E. 1976. "Petrography of the Rattlesnake Formation at the type area, central Oregon." Department of Geology and Mineral Industries, State of Oregon, Oil and Gas Investigations 25: 1-34.

Famoso, Nicholas A., and Edward Byrd Davis. 2014. "Occlusal Enamel Complexity in middle Miocene to Holocene Equids (Equidae: Perissodactyla) of North America." PLOS ONE 9 (2): 11.

Famoso, Nicholas A., Robert S. Feranec, and Edward Byrd Davis. 2013. "Occlusal enamel complexity and its implications for lophodonty, hypsodony, body mass, and diet in extinct and extant ungulates." Palaeogeography, Palaeoclimatology, Palaeoecology 387: 211-216.

Fremd, T. J. 2010. "Guidebook: SVP Field Symposium 2010. John Day Basin Field Conference." (Society of Vertebrate Paleontology) 153.

Hunt, R. M., and E. Stepleton. 2004. "Geology and paleontology of the upper John Day beds, John Day River Valley, Oregon: lithostratigraphic and biochronologic revision in the Haystack Valley and Kimberly areas (Kimberly and Mt. Misery quadrangles)." Bulletin of the American Museum of Natural History (282): 1-90.

Martin, J. E., and T. J. Fremd. 2001. "Revision of the lithostratigraphy of the Hemphillian Rattlesnake units of central Oregon." PaleoBios 21: 89.

Martin, James E. 1983. "Additions to the early Hemphillian (Miocene) Rattlesnake Fauna from central Oregon." Proceedings of the South Dakota Academy of Science 62: 23-33.

McClaughry, J. D., Ferns, M. L, M. J. Streck, K. A. Patridge, and C. L. Gordon. 2009. Paleogene calderas of central and eastern Oregon: Eruptive sources of widespread tuffs in the John Day and Clarno Formations. Vol. 15, in Volcanoes to Vineyards: Geologic Field Trips through the Dynamic Landscape of the Pacific Northwest, edited by J.E., R.J. Dorsey, and I.P. Madin O'Connor, 407-434. Geological Society of America Field Guide.

Merriam, J. C., C. Stock, and C. L. Moody. 1925. "The Pliocene Rattlesnake Formation and fauna of eastern Oregon, with notes on the geology of the Rattlesnake and Mascall deposits." Carnegie Institution of Washington, Contributions to Palaeontology 347: 43-92.

Retallack, G. J, E. A. Bestland, and T. J. Fremd. 2000. "Eocene and Oligocene paleosols of central Oregon." Geological Society of America Special Paper 344: 196.

Rytuba, J. J., and E. H. McKee. 1984. "Peralkaline ash flow tuffs and calderas of the McDermitt." Journal Geophysical Research 89: 8616-8628.

Samuels, J. X., and J. L. Cavin. 2013. "The earliest known fisher (Mustelidae), a new species from the Rattlesnake Formation of Oregon." Journal of Vertebrate Paleontology 33 (2): 1-7.

Samuels, J. X., and J. Zancanella. 2011. "An early Hemphillian occurrence of Castor (Castoridae) from the Rattlesnake Formation of Oregon." Journal of Paleontology 85: 930-935.

Samuels, J. X., L. Barry Albright III, and Theodore J. Fremd. 2015. "The Last Fossil Primate in North America, New Material of the Enigmatic Ekgmowechashala From the Arikareean of Oregon." American Journal of Physical Anthropology 158: 43-54.

Seligman, Angela N., Ilya N. Bindeman, Jason McClaughry, Richard A. Stern, and Chris Fisher. 2014. "The earliest low and high 18O caldera-forming eruptions of the Yellowstone plume: implications for the 30–40 Ma Oregon calderas and speculations on plume-triggered delaminations." Frontiers in Earth Science 2: 1-9. doi:https://doi.org/10.3389/feart.2014.00034.

1974. "Senate Report 93-1233." Washington, DC.

Tweet, Justin S., Vincent L. Santucci, and H. Gregory McDonald. 2016. "Name-bearing fossil type specimens and taxa named from National Park Service Areas." Edited by R. M. Sullivan and S. G. Lucas. New Mexico Museum of Natural History and Science Bulletin 73: 227-288.

Emery, Meaghan M., Edward B. Davis, and Samantha S. B. Hopkins. 2016. "Systematic Reassessment of an Agriochoerid Oreodont from the Hancock

Mammal Quarry, Clarno (Eocene, Duchesnean), Oregon." Journal of Vertebrate Paleontology 4634 (January): e1041970. doi:10.1080/02724634.2015 .1041970.

Robson, Selina V., Nicholas A. Famoso, Edward Byrd Davis, and Samantha S.B. Hopkins. 2019. "First Mesonychid from the Clarno Formation (Eocene) of Oregon, USA." Palaeontologia Electronica 22 (2). doi:10.26879/856.

Samuels, Joshua X., L. Barry Albright, and Theodore J. Fremd. 2015. "The Last Fossil Primate in North America, New Material of the Enigmatic Ekgmowe-chashala from the Arikareean of Oregon." American Journal of Physical Anthropology. doi:10.1002/ ajpa.22769.

Samuels, Joshua X., and William W Korth. 2017. "The First Eocene Rodents from the Pacific North-west, USA." Palaeontologia Electronica 20 (2). doi:10.26879/717.

Page 98: https://www.cityofprineville.com/wetlands

Page 116: This poem, and the poem "SONOS" on page 36, have not been previously published, though they are part of a bigger multidisciplinary project called "Open Range: Mountain Passage".

Page 119:

[1] Ralph Waldo Emerson.

[2] Asa Gray, considered the preeminent American botanist of the 19th-century and author of numerous botanical texts.

[3] Lodgepole pine (Pinus contorta).

[4] Joseph Dalton Hooker, British botanist and sometime collector and collaborator with Gray.

[5] Thoreau never came this far west. This narrative, fashioned to occur on his birthday, is not entirely implausible; he had consumption, as tuberculosis was then known, and had been counseled to go west for the dry air.

Page 151: Plants.usda.gov; Pnwflowers.com